Infinite Light planted by good souls . . .

They have begun using the image of a garden to help us understand that achieving our goals here will take constant care and tending in order to produce a great and lasting beauty. They call their world the Garden of Souls because even in the hereafter, the souls still grow in wisdom and spirituality for their own good, and for the good of us on earth. Part of the continual spiritual growth of the souls in the garden is in watching over us on earth. They will try their best to help us help ourselves by showing us the signs we need to navigate the course we are on.

—from *Walking in the Garden of Souls*

GEORGE ANDERSON

&

ANDREW BARONE

BERKLEY BOOKS
NEW YORK

WALKING
in the
GARDEN
of SOULS

George Anderson's

Advice from

the Hereafter,

for Living in

the Here and Now

Most Berkley Books are available at special quantity discounts for bulk purchases for sales promotions, premiums, fund-raising, or educational use. Special books, or book excerpts, can also be created to fit specific needs.

For details, write: Special Markets, The Berkley Publishing Group, 375 Hudson Street, New York, New York 10014.

*In some instances, names and personal details in this book have been changed
to protect the privacy of the individual or family.*

A Berkley Book
Published by The Berkley Publishing Group
A division of Penguin Putnam Inc.
375 Hudson Street
New York, New York 10014

PRINTING HISTORY
G. P. Putnam's Sons hardcover edition / October 2001
Berkley trade paperback edition / October 2002

Berkley trade paperback ISBN: 0-425-18611-3

The Library of Congress has catalogued the G. P. Putnam's Sons hardcover edition as follows:

Anderson, George (George P.)
Walking in the garden of souls : George Anderson's advice
from the hereafter, for the living in the here and now /
George Anderson & Andrew Barone.
p. cm.
ISBN 0-399-14790-X
I. Spiritualism. 2. Future life. I. Barone, Andrew.
II. Title.
BF1290.A48   2001   2001034921
133.9—dc21

PRINTED IN THE UNITED STATES OF AMERICA

10 9 8 7 6 5

This book is dedicated to my mother, Eleanor Anderson, for giving me the gift of her simple spirituality, and to bereaved parents everywhere whose young angels make the hereafter a beautiful place for me to visit.

—GEORGE ANDERSON

This book is also dedicated with love to Andrew and Victoria Petrone, who have planted such joy in my garden.

—ANDREW BARONE

CONTENTS

WALKING
in the
GARDEN
of SOULS

WALKING in
the GARDEN
of SOULS

The souls in the hereafter have been at it again.

January of 1996 is a rather unremarkable month in the memory of most people. It would have also been for me, but two rather remarkable things happened to make it stand out in my mind. The first happened when snow chose that month to tumble out of the gray sky in feet rather than inches, and then froze, turning New York into a city of crystal. The second remarkable thing came courtesy of those amazing souls in the hereafter. Amid the magical opulence of all that glistening snow, they found an opportunity to send another portrait of their universe, like a message in a bottle, to the earth. The opportunity came via a soul, reaching out to a loved one here, who explained the world of the here-after in a way the souls had never done before. It was a curious anal-ogy—so simple that even we on the earth can understand, yet so profound that it could explain perfectly why life is the way it is, both here *and* hereafter. Life, the soul explained, is like a *garden*—a magnifi-cent Garden of Souls. What is planted by us in this lifetime will bloom for us in a life to come.

One particularly snowy day that January found us hovering around the phone in our office. The brave people who actually made it into work were now waiting anxiously for clients to cancel their appointments due to the inclement weather, so that they could go home before the roads got any worse. Everyone scheduled to attend an appointment that day had canceled, except for the five o'clock appointment, who had yet to call us to say they couldn't attempt the trip out to Long Island. We waited, waited some more, and then tried calling. There was no answer, which meant they actually might have been foolhardy enough to brave the bad weather. Just in case they actually made it, I and my assistant decided to stay and make sure they wouldn't show up to an empty office. We waited, watching the snow turn to ice as the day got darker and colder.

At about ten minutes past five o'clock, a young couple appeared in the lobby, wet and cold. The woman looked barely out of her teens, and her hair was dripping and matted to her face. The young man was about the same age and just as wet. They explained to me that they could not get a taxi to travel all the way here, so the driver took them as far as he was able, which was three blocks short of our location. They walked the rest of the way. I asked the young woman why she didn't just cancel if the going was so tough, but she responded resolutely, "There is some-thing I need to know—I *need* to have this happen." That was good enough for me, so we put their coats on the radiator to dry, gave them each a towel, and I began the session.

The souls seemed to move lazily through the beginning of the session, as if they were unsure as to who was going to communicate first. It felt as if they were stalling for time. One female presence seemed to drift into my focus, but she remained shadowy and tentative, as if not wanting to step any closer to us. She would have to come more into focus before I could understand her communication, so I waited for another soul to begin reaching out. An uncle and grandfather soon followed and began communicating to the young woman. The messages seemed to me rather innocuous and mundane, but the young woman listened intently to their communication. As I related their messages, my own feelings began to creep into my thoughts: this young woman, with her bright smile and sweet disposition, didn't seem old enough to have sustained any substantial tragedy. I was quite mistaken. Before I could even finish the thought, my mind was interrupted by the words, *"I'm ashamed."*

"What?" The words rang in my ears so clearly I thought they came from within the room.

"What?" the young woman asked me, confused.

"She says she's ashamed."

"Who?" the young man asked.

"Wait a minute," I told them. I listened more carefully to the soul communicating. She seemed to inch closer, as if testing the ground before her to make sure it was safe. "She says this is *Mother*, and she says she's ashamed." What I thought was water from the young woman's wet hair was actually the tears that came down her face in a sudden flood.

"Ask her why this is *happening*," she pleaded, wiping her tears with the towel.

"Let's let her go at her own pace," I cautioned her. The communication is always better when the souls are prompted by their own need to speak. The soul, who at first was so tenuous, now moved gradually closer to reach out to the young woman. "She says to me, '*This is my daughter*.' She keeps telling me to tell you she is so sorry. She is ashamed of her behavior on the earth." The young woman nodded in agreement, so I continued. "There is another female presence there with her . . . very young, a baby girl."

She didn't respond, so I looked up to make sure she understood. As I caught sight of her face, I noticed that her eyes were as wide as saucer plates, and she looked terrified. The young man next to her put his head in his hands and began to cry. The soul asked me to continue, however. "And she says, '*I am still your child. You did nothing wrong*.'"

As the session went on, the soul of the young woman's mother told the difficult story of her own mental illness on the earth, her inability to cope with her daughter, and the neglect this young woman was made to suffer as a child. Eventually, the young woman married the gentleman seated next to her in the session—both, literally, to escape the dysfunctional houses they grew up in. Although they were just teenagers, they wanted to start a family right away and shower a child with the love they never felt they got as children themselves. A few months after they were married, they were expecting a child.

A few months into the young woman's pregnancy, her mother passed on from the effects of alcohol abuse. The young woman's feelings of freedom from her mother's cruelty and madness gave way to an obsessive fear that she was destined to become just like her, thinking she would also fall victim to the same mental illness and alcoholism that plagued her mother's distraught life. She began worrying constantly that she would not be a good mother, and had terrible thoughts of history repeating the same circumstances she lived through as a child. No matter how much her husband tried to console and reason with her, the fear grew worse each day. One night, in her fifth month of pregnancy, the young woman woke up in terrible pain. A few hours later, she had lost her unborn baby.

I understand on many levels why it is so important for the souls to reach out to us and change the direction of our thinking. This young woman came to the session feeling she was being punished somehow—that God's way of protecting her baby from cruelty was to take it from her. She thought she killed her baby by not wanting it badly enough. The ironic thing is that no matter how rough a relationship this young woman had with her mother, she knew her mother was the only person who could be counted on to tell her the straight truth about why she was being punished, and whether God would ever allow her to be a mother.

In the session, her mother apologized for her abuse, and told her daughter how difficult it was to see her Life Review in the hereafter, watching her cruelty to such a lovely, smiling little girl. But she was ill, she explained, and although she loved her daughter, her life had become a maze of incoherence and fear that she could not find a way out of. In the hereafter, she was now learning to reconcile what she did on the earth through the grace and love of the Infinite Light. Part of that reconciliation now was to help her daughter to understand. The mother explained how surprised she was to find that her own choices and circumstances on the earth were like seeds that she was unknowingly planting throughout her life. *"Nothing would grow with the seeds I planted on the earth, no matter how hard I tried,"* she explained. *"I just didn't understand it. It wasn't until I passed on that I found all the seeds in my life became a garden for me in the hereafter, and all my hope, all my sanity, and all my peace was blooming there."*

The end of the session was a poignant example of the power of love. The young woman's mother communicated to us that she was grateful for her daughter's forgiveness. She was proud of the woman her daughter had become, and the wonderful mother she knew her daughter would soon be. It was now time for her to forgive herself for losing her own child. The mother told us that she was beginning to understand her life in a way that never made sense on the earth. She also explained that everything that happened to her daughter on the earth was like a seed that is planted, which will become a beautiful garden for her in the hereafter. *"Your forgiveness of me is like a flower that bloomed for me here,"* she told us. *"It will bloom for you also, when your time has come."*

Both young people wiped away tears as the mother communicated to them how proud she was that the hard circumstances they endured had not ruined their hope. It was time for both mother and daughter to release the years of pain and anguish, and to look at life as an opportunity to make love grow, both now and later. *"You have not lost your daughter,"* she told the couple before leaving at the end of the session, *"She is with me in my garden. You will have more children to love and be loved by. You go on in peace as we will. Your daughter and I will always be here for you. When you feel yourself losing hope, just think of us here, hand in hand, walking in the garden of souls."*

1.

THERE IS *a* GARDEN

Imagine your life. Imagine your life, not as it is now and not how it used to be, but imagine your life the way love songs, fairy tales, and bedtime stories told you it was going to be. Imagine waking up one fine morning from a soft bed into luminous sunlight, beginning each day feeling warm, well fed, well loved and well cared for. Imagine moving effortlessly through your day, surrounded by the people you love, working at a job that brings you a sense of such joy and accomplishment that you love being in service to others. Imagine returning home at the end of your lovely day to a beautiful warm house filled with the smiling faces of those you truly love, where there are good things to eat and evenings are spent by a glorious fire, laughing with careless abandon. Imagine drifting outside and walking under a star-filled sky where fireflies dance in the warm breeze. Imagine walking in a beautiful garden—just over a hill of constant torment, past the rocks of hurt and anger, over the brook of constant worry, past the weeds of intolerance and hatred, to a place of such perfect peace that even the ground feels soft and receptive beneath your feet. The fire of true love can be rekindled there by a carpet of heather, and reconciliation with the past can happen in an open field of understanding, lit by a golden sun of forgiveness. Turmoil and anguish disappear under a shady tree. Trouble never lived here and peace will never leave. No one ever grows old, no one ever becomes ill, and no one ever dies. Welcome to the world of the hereafter—welcome to the Garden of Souls.

There is a Garden of Souls. It is not only a real and vibrant place, but it is also closer than we can imagine. It is where we once lived, and it is also where we will return. It is a place we will see again only after our lifetime of struggle, hardship and hurt has earned us the reward of true and final peace. The Garden waits for all of us who have the courage to travel the bumpy and crooked roads of the earth until they eventually broaden, smooth out, and lead us there. It is a place of unusual beauty and peace, where the love and understanding that somehow eluded us on the earth can be found as abundant as the oxygen we breathe. It is a place where not only our loved ones who have passed on live and grow, but also a place where our lost hopes and dreams will be absorbed and recycled, after having been tossed by cruel circumstance from the earth. Even though we have no conscious recollection of it now, we were once born of this world and we understood it well. Even though we may not feel it now, we were once children in the Garden of Souls with hearts filled with love and peace. But living on the earth, we have become so easily disarmed by the circumstances of life here and the struggles we have to endure, that our disappointment and despair have eroded the memory of that place and diminished in our hearts the wonderful light from the Garden. The longer we live on the earth, the more life circumstances drain the reserves of the peace and love we had before our journey here began. We live on, we get older, we experience pain, we endure tragedy—our hearts harden, our peace disappears, and our souls no longer remember why we are here. We forget that we are on the earth to learn strength in our adversity, to learn peace in our struggle, to learn joy in our sorrow—to *learn*. This is the understanding that leads us to knowledge, and our knowledge that leads us back to the Garden—back to our home.

We are all human, and in our humanness we tend to regard any trouble that comes our way as a personal attack against us—against our happiness. We work and work, trying to be the people we *think* will win us a place in the hereafter, but our work is done more out of fear rather than actual understanding of why we must face struggle. Life tears on, we watch loved ones, opportunities, and happiness slip like sand through our fingers, and we become disillusioned—we begin wandering aimlessly through perhaps the most important learning experiences of our lives.

Our fall from our purpose here has not escaped the notice of the souls in the hereafter, who by their very caring nature are concerned for our spiritual lives. They know very well that the difficulties we endure while we are on the earth—and how we cope with and overcome them—will be perhaps the toughest test of our faith and spirit. They also know that these trials are a necessary part of our lives in order to fulfill the goals we had set for ourselves when we last left the Garden. The souls know and they understand, because they themselves were once part of the challenge of life on earth. They remember from their *own* experiences here that hope, understanding, and acceptance are lessons that may take a lifetime to learn. Now that they have entered the Garden, and their struggles have paid off so handsomely, they want to help us keep to our purpose here, so that we can share in the reward of returning to the Garden when it is our time to return.

IN A GARDEN PAST

We were once a much more spiritual planet. A few thousand years ago, we understood and accepted without question that we were governed by a power much greater than our own. Our lives were spent in service to that power with the promise of greater things to come. We understood that we could tap into that power when it was needed to survive, and we gave back to that same power from our own abundance when fate richly rewarded us. In a garden not so long ago, we recognized that each of us had this power of the Infinite Light within us, and we spent our time on the earth living and working to be considered worthy of such a precious gift. It was also an extraordinary time when we could acknowledge that prophets walked among us on the earth—Christ, Buddha, Joan of Arc, Mohammed, and countless others—who were so pure of spiritual purpose that the light of the Garden of Souls flickered in their eyes.

But then something odd happened. In all our education, we had gotten too wise for our own good. As in the biblical story of Adam and Eve, we gained in knowledge, only to lose heavily in the purity of our souls. The world became much smaller when viewed from an airplane, and the heavens that once produced such awe in us were now being surveyed regularly with satellites. The mysticism of the spiritual things we held precious on the earth were now being explained and discounted wholesale by science and technology. We concluded in those fateful years that perhaps God did not live in the heavens, and perhaps did not even reside near the earth. We had checked and tested and searched, and God was nowhere to be found.

The many years that followed were perhaps the darkest for our spirituality on the earth. Like so many insignificant rulers throughout history, we decided as a people that *we* were God, and life was all about *us*. Our existence on earth, flawed and damaged though it was, became our heaven, and the only reward for a life well spent was a life well spent. Those who were less than us, or weaker, or slower, were discarded. If tragedy found us, we were eliminated from the minds and hearts of others and forgotten. Like spoiled children, we threw away the things we could not easily understand, and embraced anything that would distract us from the discomfort of hopelessness. For a long time afterward, belief in any spirituality seemed silly and small-minded, and we cast ourselves adrift in a sea of self-gratification and lack of accountability. Things were easier that way, and it felt better—no more having to worry about anyone else but ourselves, no reason to love and no reason to care. We could only create, at best, a makeshift reward of contentedness from our folly of self-indulgence. Like all unearned rewards, it was garish and hollow, and we found our only prize for this futile work to be a well-fed mind in a starved soul.

How patient the Infinite Light is with us. We had fallen so far from our purpose, and life had become unworthy of living. All our technology and miracles of science could not feed the hungry, or clothe the poor, or bring any sense of peace to our hearts. We were spiritually bankrupt in a world that had become more violent by the day, and more than once in our history were we in real danger of actually ceasing to exist. But the souls, who sent signals to us in earnest, only to watch them fall unheard and unnoticed, had never left us. They knew that with every blight comes a correction, and eventually, the pendulum that swung so far to one direction would eventually come back the other way. In my more than forty years of listening to the souls in the hereafter and their incredible words of hope to their love ones here, I have found that the souls are patient to a fault. They know it must be *our* idea to listen to them, and they are willing to wait until their message of hope begins taking root in our hearts. The message of these kind and loving souls is as simple as this: we, each of us, must create a Garden on the earth while we are here.

IN A GARDEN PRESENT

We are living at the dawn of the most spiritual age the earth has seen. In my own lifetime I have noticed significant changes to people everywhere, in both heart and mind. Some of the seeds from the Garden have fallen in our path, and we are beginning to allow them to take root within us. Whether it is because we want to or because we have to, we are changing, and reckoning with the possibility that there may very well be a happy ending to the story of our life on earth. Whether or not we had intended it to be this way is of no consequence—we now have nowhere else left to walk but forward, toward the light of hope. How pleased the souls must be—they have been watching us from a distant garden, and know we are beginning to listen with our hearts and not with our pride. Ideas in religion, belief in life hereafter, and firsthand accounts from people who have seen the Garden of Souls with their own eyes are not laughed at or ridiculed as they were as little as twenty-five years ago. More people want to believe than scoff, and it has been estimated that now nearly one third of the population of this planet believes without question in the existence of life hereafter. This must be very good news for the souls there—to be considered to actually exist.

Never in any time in my life have I seen such a strong need for spiritual fulfillment as in the past few years. Maybe we have lost the arrogance that tells us *we* are the center of the universe, or maybe it is the admission that surviving without hope and peace is not surviving at all. I believe that more of us have begun unplugging our ears, and have actually heard the souls and realize their willingness to help us to understand. Our goal here is a simple one: we have come here with our fear, with our shortcomings, with our impatience and with our intolerance, to learn how to create a Garden on the earth. We have foolishly burned our field and gone hungry more than once before in the history of humankind, but now we are taking the slow steps of learning how to cultivate a garden that will feed our spiritual needs as well as the needs of others on the earth. The Infinite Light's hope for us is that we can look past the failings of our lives and the lives of those around us, and *use* our experiences to fill a garden with the only tools we will ever need— love and hope.

Life here is not like the well-ordered garden of souls in the hereafter, and for very good reason. In the world of the hereafter, the diseases of the soul, like hate, violence, lack of compassion, and hopelessness, do not exist. There is no need for the souls to experience these things, since they have learned well from their own struggles during their life on earth. But just as it was for the souls of friends and loved ones before us, our graduation from this world to the next will be the cure our souls so desperately need. While we are here, we will be inundated with opportunities to do wrong so that we can learn what is right. The souls have constantly told me in one way or another, *"If you knew the answers, it wouldn't be a test. Learn to listen to the voices all around you, especially the one in your heart."* There are signs all around us which point the direction to where we must walk. Human nature is such that unless a sign slaps us squarely in the face, it is very easily missed. It is up to us to find the signs that will create the map that is to be our journey on the earth. Sometimes signs come in the form of kindness from strangers, and sometimes in the cruelty of those we know well. But these necessary experiences shape us into the people we must be for ourselves and for one another. What we do while we are on the earth—who we are and how we handle ourselves in the experiences we find ourselves in—measures what we are to gain from having lived life here.

The souls are communicating to us in a way they have never done before. Perhaps it is because they know we are beginning to listen. They have begun using the image of a garden to help us understand that achieving our goals here will take constant care and tending in order to produce a great and lasting beauty. They call their world the Garden of Souls because even in the hereafter, the souls still grow in wisdom and spirituality for their own good, and for the good of those they care for on the earth. Although their garden is free of the trials and troubles that plague the earth, their garden grows even greater by helping us to plant a garden of our own on the earth. As the souls help us with our garden, they see the fruits of their labor in the peace and hope that blooms on the earth. It brings the souls joy without measure to help us to help ourselves create a garden of peace and understanding on the earth.

Think of your life. Think of your life, not as you thought it would be, but think of your life the way you live it now. Think of the love that has been buried under piles of broken trust. Think of the impatience you show to people who appear weaker, or slower, or poorer, or less fortunate. Think of the struggles that have crafted the hard shell of fear that you live within. Think of the tragedies you have endured that bring you to your hands and knees, searching for hope that has fallen from your heart and has been scattered by an unsympathetic wind. We need more than ever to listen to the messages of hope that are so freely given by the Infinite Light and the souls in the hereafter, who want so much for us to understand how beautiful their garden is. They want so much to show us how beautiful our garden can be. They want so much to help us sow the seeds of peace and hope on the earth so that each of us can have a garden of our own. They know it is possible, and they know from their own experiences on the earth that it will require work. But they know that the result will be a garden beyond our wildest imagination.

IN A GARDEN TO COME

Part of the continual spiritual growth of the souls in the Garden is in watching over us on the earth. They will try their best to help us help *ourselves*, by showing us the signs we need to navigate the course we are on. The souls understand that everything we will experience in our lifetime is another brick in the path that takes us to a garden of peace, but we have to walk that road with only our faith in ourselves, our lives, and the Infinite Light as our guide. The souls know it is the hardest thing we will ever do on the earth—to walk ahead without clear rules—but they know from their own experience what things may come if we can only hold on to our hope that their *is* a Garden just ahead of us. They also know that for all the guidance they try to give us from that unique vantage point, they can only bring us to the river of understanding and peace, but they cannot make us drink from it. What we make of our lifetime here will be entirely up to us. Still, undaunted, they will tirelessly shower the earth with seeds of hope from the Garden, in the form of their messages and whisperings to us on the earth. They know that in time, one day, one by one, each of us will open that hard shell of fear just enough to let their words of hope find their way to our ears. Listen carefully, the souls have told us—there is a Garden.

The ultimate path to the Infinite Light runs directly through our own garden of hope. Life on the earth is more a voyage of self-discovery than it is a discovery of people and things around us. The more we learn about ourselves, the more we understand the world around us. The more things we live through, the more we can decipher our own motivations here and effect change in ourselves and those around us. That having been said, it is also possible that we might never fully understand the complexities of our purpose here—the things that we must do and the things that we must be for each other—but I have been made certain by the souls and their messages that there is a purpose so compelling that it is worth every second of our attention. While we are here, we will create so many of the struggles we endure, but they do have a meaning and a purpose—it will be up to us to recognize it. It is easy to look backward from the circumstances in our lives to understand the method to the madness that made us who we must be while we are here. The real trick, of course, is to look *ahead* with the same kind of understanding and plot the future of our learning experiences, having remembered the pain of the past, yet all the while still clinging to the hope of better things to come.

I imagine that each one of us, in time, will experience a moment of clarity when everything that has circled around us misunderstood lands finally in a perfect field of reason in our hearts. We will understand why it is so important to *live* while we are on the earth. It is at the souls' insistence that we write this book—they need their message to be heard, and not just by me and some fortunate families who have heard these messages directly from their loved ones. The souls know that it is time that we come to the realization that we must begin our garden while we can—time is moving and the seasons are becoming shorter. What we cultivate in the winter of our lives on the earth will burst forth in the spring of our understanding. We are capable of creating a garden on earth, if we are willing to work at it.

Imagine your life. Imagine your life, not as it is now and not how it was, but imagine your life the way the souls promise it can be if we can take just one more leap of faith and trust what the souls are tying to tell each of us. We can all hear them if we listen, even if some can hear them better than others. Some who are filled with the deafening noise of anger and hurt will have to strain to hear. Others will have to listen past the low drone of inner turmoil, but the souls will be heard. Allow their words to help you build a garden on the earth. It is why we are here. Work done in the garden of your own soul can produce such abundance that it will carry over to others, into your life, and into your life hereafter. Our mission on the earth is simple—to leave behind a garden of our own making on the earth, before we return and find ourselves walking once again with those we love in the magnificent Garden of Souls.

2.

THE LIFE *of* *a* MEDIUM

In the early 1980s I did a cable television show called "Psychic Channels," which, looking back, was revolutionary for its time. It was more or less a televised version of the groups I still do on a regular basis—connecting the souls in the hereafter with their grieving loved ones here. I was outside the studio one afternoon going to my car after a taping, and a woman about twenty feet away stopped and addressed her two friends in a voice loud enough for me to hear. *"Look girls,"* she said, laughing. *"There's George Anderson—small medium at large."* I found the play on words very funny and laughed along with them, not realizing until much later, when it was pointed out to me, that the joke was at my expense. Even after it was explained to me that I was being made fun of, I still found nothing wrong with someone easing their own fear of my ability to communicate with the souls in the hereafter by taking a potshot at me. The thought of physical death and life after this one is still disconcerting to many people, and if dismissing my work as "a crock" would make someone feel better or ease their mind about the inevitable, I don't mind, and neither do the souls in the hereafter.

My life is not normal, but I have lived long enough and heard enough circumstances, good and bad, to understand that "normal" is truly a relative term. The thing that makes me "abnormal" to some people makes me "unique" to others. My life being so far from normal has not always been easy, but it certainly has been interesting and quite educational. Once I accepted that it was my differences that made me who I am, I learned to work with what I had and to be proud of my accomplishments. In time, and with the souls' help, I realized that there is a reason and purpose to why we are created the way we are. Some of us have physical differences, some have emotional or environmental differences, but these differences create who we are and who we will be. But it is how we use this uniqueness in impacting the world around us that helps form our spiritual experiences on the earth. In the whole scheme of things here and hereafter, *uniqueness* is a gift, and *different* is not so bad after all.

I began seeing the souls in the hereafter and hearing them communicate at the age of six, after a bout with chicken pox turned into encephalomyelitis (a swelling of the brain) and briefly paralyzed my legs. As I got better, the souls began appearing. They came slowly at first, with the appearance of a woman I called "Lilac Lady" because she always appeared in a lilac-colored haze, followed by others, like the relatives of friends, or the saints and extraordinary people I recognized from my religious education. Their appearances became a regular and welcome event in my young life. I liked hearing from them because they made me feel safe, and they understood me like no one else could. I saw nothing unusual about their appearances and actually looked forward to hearing from them, until I found out that no one else experienced visitations or heard messages. I was often ridiculed for the things I saw and heard, to the point where it became a real problem for my parents and teachers. To add to this peculiar problem, I also happened to be very small for my age and was too shy to make friends with other children. I was picked on mercilessly in school for the things I said, and as I moved from grade to grade, my handful of friends trickled down to none. The only thing I had that was positive in my life was the relationship I had with these extraordinary souls who visited with me when I was hurt or upset. They came and listened to my feelings, and I could speak to them from my heart, without even having to say the words out loud. I eventually found myself retreating from the actual world of people on the earth and into a world where these wonderful souls knew and loved me, and spoke to me like I had real value to them. After a while, I had no use for the outside world and fought having to be part of it every chance I could. For a time, I was even tutored at home. It was a blessing to be able to stay far from the impatient, unforgiving world outside.

By my teenage years, I was thought of by just about everyone as having mental problems. Even most family members and the few friends I still had decided that I was slightly bonkers. Although I was never diagnosed with a mental illness, I do believe in retrospect that my shying away from the physical world and into the world of the souls was a type of emotional problem. As I grew into my teens, the pressure to fit in with the other teenagers was almost overpowering—I just wanted to be like everyone else. I no longer wanted to hear the voices that once comforted me. The ability that once felt so reassuring now became a burden and a constant reminder that I was different. The last thing you want to be when you are a teenager is *different*, and I found myself resisting my ability to hear the souls and hoping they would just disappear. I entered my late teens, my small world started widening, and I found myself having less and less use for those words that came from the souls who tried to guide and shape my life. I also discovered that I could tune them out or listen to them at will—a nifty trick I had never realized before. Apparently this ability had a "mute" button, which I found myself pressing more and more. I found myself a part-time job in a shoe store, and now had pin money in my pocket and a small circle of friends. Things started to change—I knew it, and I think the souls knew it too. They began coming less and less frequently at about the same time that I found myself maturing into a young adult. I didn't miss them—I began to resent the fact that so many of my problems with other people were because of these damn souls. Now, whenever the souls would appear I would ignore them. Still, they came with hope and love, but I wouldn't listen. Like every other young adult with a small taste of freedom, I decided I didn't need anybody to invade my thoughts and navigate my actions. I wanted to do things on my own now, without the hand-holding and encouragement from those souls who now seemed to me so parochial and old-fashioned. I didn't want this ability that caused me so much heartache anymore, so I decided to bury it—bury it with a shovel, and then bury the shovel. I made the conscious decision to stop listening, in the hope that with no one to listen to them, the souls would move on. For once, I felt in control of my own life, and the souls retreated slowly without a fight. Although I could still feel them around, they were easy to ignore since they no longer spoke or appeared. Finally, I thought, I am free, I could be my own man.

One of the things that life has taught me in my maturity is that young adults believe they are invincible and the world revolves around them. What a wonderful thing to feel, but unfortunately, it comes at the wrong point in our lives. It is a shame we couldn't feel that way when we are in the middle age of our lives—when we start to feel as if we are an insignificant piece of a very big puzzle, or when we realize that lack of hope is a large, unyielding stone that could crush us at any time. Still, I am grateful to have felt like a brimming fountain of dreams at least once in my life, when things were in my control, and the only voice in my head was actually mine. I graduated college and found a job at the New York Telephone Company as an operator—an irony I did not comprehend until much later. I had a small circle of good friends with whom I shared a warped sense of humor and a passion for old movies. Even though I was broke nearly all the time, life was exciting because I was the only one in the driver's seat, and I made all the decisions, good and bad, for myself.

THE BEGINNING OF THE BEGINNING

Throughout my life as a teenager, and then as a young adult, I could still feel the current of communication lines that had never really closed between myself and the hereafter, but I fought it rather the same way that a child that puts his hands over his ears and sings the "Star-Spangled Banner" when he doesn't want to hear something someone else seems intent on him hearing. I was a young adult in the 1970s when everything was being tried for the first time—even the supernatural, ESP, and the like. I suppose I was about as interested as the next guy in these phenomena, but was more interested in the fact that people were accepting without question the fact that things like this could happen. I did feel a small sense of vindication—that perhaps I was not crazy after all, but it wasn't enough to join the psychic parade and tell people that I could hear from the "other side," the new catch-phrase for the souls in the hereafter. Still, not wanting to reopen the Pandora's Box that I so desperately tried to keep shut, I invented a new life history that did not include any voices or visions. Once in a while, at a party or in a group, people marveled at my apparently clever sense of mind reading or predictions—things that would slip through the cracks of my consciousness and pop up unexpectedly without my control. It was okay though—some people thought it was cool, and others thought it was a joke.

It wasn't until 1973 that I was able to really understand why it was so important for the souls to communicate, and how their messages could alter the way people thought about their circumstances. I never understood the value of the messages because I had never seen the effects of these hopeful messages on anyone else but myself, and didn't think that anyone could possibly benefit from hearing what the souls had to say. As in every other time in my life, the souls found the perfect circumstance to illustrate to me the importance of their messages and their need to communicate to their loved ones here. And for the first time since they started appearing to me, I had the good sense to really listen to their words and see the impact they could make on life here.

Years ago, I worked with a girl named Debby. She was a recent new-lywed with a wicked sense of humor and an outgoing personality. I admired her ease with people and her fun nature, and in time we talked more and more on our breaks and slow times on the job. We became best buddies, talking about everything under the sun, including her hopes and dreams for her new life with her husband. Even though Debby was high spirited and always laughing, I always got the sense that there was something in her life that caused her some pain, but it was buried under a great sense of humor and an easy smile. The only time I ever noticed that Debby was uneasy was when her husband, Brent, would meet us after work, when a bunch of the other coworkers went out for drinks. Her husband was very quiet, and when Debby was with him, she seemed different, too—more reserved and much less frenetic than at work.

A few months into our friendship, Debby invited me over for pizza after work. I needed to stop off at my apartment to change, and told Debby I would meet her and Brent in an hour at their home. When I got there, Debby answered the door. She seemed uneasy, but she worked hard to laugh and joke with me even though it was obvious that something was on her mind. By the time I had gotten there, the pizza had already arrived, but there was no sign of Brent. "Brent's going to be a while," she said, "so why don't we just go ahead and dig in?" We sat down in the living room to talk and eat pizza, but Debby seemed out of sorts and more restless. I asked her if everything was all right, but she assured me she was fine. As I ate my pizza, I looked up suddenly to see someone standing behind Debby, with her hands on Debby's shoulders. It was a woman, standing so serenely, looking down at Debby with love and admiration. I was transfixed by what I saw, and stared at the woman until Debby shook me from my trance.

"What??" she asked me, laughing. "Is there food on my face?"

"There's a woman standing behind you. She says she's Mom."

"What?" she asked me, suddenly serious. "Are you kidding?"

I could not take my eyes off this loving vision of the woman who spoke so patiently. "No, not your mom—she says mother-*in-law*." I expected Debby to tell me I was crazy, but she looked at me squarely and seriously. "What does she want?"

"She says she's near you, and that she understands. She is Brent's mom, and she's expressing concern for his well-being." I continued, knowing that the fallout from this might lose me a friend, but I felt compelled by this soul to continue. "She's talking about drug abuse by her son . . . she's concerned, but she understands."

I saw Debby's face darken and her eyes fill with tears. "What else can she tell you?" she asked me, trying to hold back her emotion.

"She says he's going through a crisis, that he's a little boy trapped in a man's body. She's not judging him, but she says that you know you need to help him to grow up and see how much there is to lose if he doesn't stop." Debby listened intently. "She also tells me that even though you didn't meet on the earth, she thinks of you as a daughter and she's proud of you for putting up with his *b.s.*"

Debby started to cry. "Tell her thanks," she said, wiping her nose.

"She already heard you," I told her. As quickly as the soul appeared, she disappeared.

I suddenly found myself gripped with fear as I began worrying how Debby would react to what I just told her, but she just sat there, staring at me. "That was incredible," she said simply. "Thank you. How long have you been able to do that?"

"For a while now," I told her, sheepishly.

"Wow. *Thank you.*" She wiped her eyes one more time, and the smile suddenly returned to her face—the outgoing Debby I knew was returning. She knocked me in the shoulder and smiled. "Wow," she said, laughing. I picked up my pizza again and we continued eating—this time, in silence.

I didn't stay at Debby's much longer after that, and I was probably as itchy to leave as Debby was itchy to have me leave so she could think about what had gone on. I understand—it was a lot to absorb, both for her and for me. I suddenly found myself full of energy after the communication from her mother-in-law, so when I got home, I parked my car and found myself just walking around Lindenhurst, Long Island. I had heard from the souls many times, but I had never seen their messages bring about that kind of reaction in another human being. It was as if the words from Debby's mother-in-law unlocked a door to the pain she tried so hard to hide from the world. I came to realize through Debby that it wasn't so much the communication, but the acknowledgment that she was not alone in her worry about her husband. At the very point she thought no one was listening to her, the mother-in-law she did not even know assured her that not only was she listening, but she was also trying to help. Something changed in Debby after that night, but the dynamic of our friendship also changed. I wish I could say that everything about our friendship changed for the good, but it didn't. While we were still the best of buddies and still went out on a frequent basis, I was not just "crazy little George" anymore—there was a distinct bit of respect for me now that I never really expected or even wanted. She told me on the last day I worked with her—several years later, and well after I started working as a medium on a regular basis—that she never would forget the feeling of knowing, no matter what happened on the earth, that she would never be alone in her pain. That small bit of communication had a profound affect on Brent as well. Shortly after that evening, shaken by hearing the concern his mother had, he entered into a treatment program, and is drug free to this day. I couldn't help but marvel at the fact that so few words meant so much when someone is in pain, and there is a reason why the souls need to reach out. Once again, they were right all along, and the more I trusted them, the more they began to communicate, and I found myself being referred to on Long Island as "the guy who can talk to the dead."

FOLLOWING THE PATH

After the impromptu session with Debby, and for a few months afterward, I had to think long and hard about the fact that everything in my life began to point to helping people make communication with their loved ones in the hereafter. I began seeing and hearing from all the "regulars" of my childhood—St. Theresa, St. Joseph, and even some of the relatives I knew who had passed on in recent years. While their appearances were random, their messages were the same—to follow the path that I found myself set upon. As if by coincidence, loved ones of people I met on the earth started appearing, as if to illustrate the need for their loved ones to hear from them. I would go to the park and see the soul of a young mother hovering over the child being pushed by her father in a swing. *"Let him know how proud I am and what a good father he has become. Tell him I will love his next wife just as much as he will,"* she said. I would go to a supermarket and see the soul of the unborn daughter of the checkout girl saying, *"Tell her it's okay, I understand. She'll have another chance. Tell her."* Fear kept me from talking to strangers about their loss, but those resourceful souls in the hereafter had an antidote for that also—suddenly friends started asking me about the strange phenomenon Debby witnessed. I saw that as the perfect opportunity to really see what was on the minds of the souls, so I would throw out whatever I saw and heard, and gauge by people's reactions whether the information being passed along was important to them, or even accurate, for that matter.

It's funny that in all the time that I have been hearing and seeing the souls from the hereafter, I never once thought it might be a figment of my imagination, as was thought by just about everyone else when I was young. For me, the images were too real, and the communication too quantifiable to think that it was somehow a product of my own making.

Sometimes messages didn't mean very much to me, but to my friends, they were answers to the questions they hid in the quiet of their hearts. Sometimes the relief they felt was overwhelming for them, as if a heavy burden was removed from their shoulders, and I found through these sessions that the need for peace far outweighed my need for proof that the souls knew what they were doing. But the more the souls communicated, the more I tested them. I wanted to read for people whose loss I did not know about, to see how, why, and in what order their loved ones came through. Then, through subsequent sessions, I barred questions from the sitter—it would be up to their loved ones to answer the questions that had not yet been asked. Again, and true to form, the souls knew exactly how to communicate to their loved ones without the sitter having to ask anything about them.

I should have been happy that I was able to prove to my own satisfaction that the souls were, in fact, communicating their messages of hope to their loved ones here. I thought of it as a kind of miracle—our loved ones never really leave us, and we are never alone on the earth no matter how alone we feel sometimes. I found a new sense of respect for the souls who communicated so thoughtfully for the friends, friends of friends, and now strangers who came to me on a regular basis. I should have been happy, but I wasn't. The more I allowed myself to be the voice of the souls in the hereafter, the more frightened of it I became. This was a *miracle*, and I was a fool. I had no business communicating these messages to people in varying states of grief and hopelessness, because I was not a good enough person—not good enough to be part of their most personal grief, and not good enough to represent the wonderful souls who care so much about us that they will punch a hole in this dimension to help us understand that all is not lost to death.

I started having nightmares, the kind of nightmares that send you to school in your underwear. There were also nightmares about being trusted to hold precious stones for someone, only to find that they had slipped out of a hole in my pocket. The responsibility of communicating for the souls, as well as the responsibility of doing my absolute best for the people who came to hear the communication, began to weigh very heavily on my conscience. I started to feel that I was trusted with something I was not strong enough or smart enough to handle, and that eventually my incompetence was going to hurt a lot of people. I worried that the trust people were placing in my ability, both here and hereafter, was something that I did not earn. I didn't feel qualified to take on the responsibility of holding in my hands what little hope people had left after their losses. During the sessions, though, I felt so exhilarated by the energy the souls were transmitting, and the people here were so grateful for the opportunity to hear the words from their loved ones in the hereafter, that it was difficult to reconcile my feelings at the end of the day. Listening to the souls communicate about the different aspects of life, like suicide, abortion, terminal illness, and the like were beginning to change just about every thought I had about life here. But the more I learned, however, the less worthy I felt. I began feeling as if the souls picked the wrong emissary on the earth, mostly because I had a hard time accepting some of the things they communicated, and an even harder time relating the information to a grief-stricken person in front of me. I found myself in the middle of a session, questioning the souls who were communicating, because I could not accept the information they were transmitting. This was especially true when a woman, whose young daughter was murdered by her abusive boyfriend, came to me at the end of her hope to hear from her daughter. The girl was only nineteen when she was murdered in a fit of jealous rage by her boyfriend, who later took his own life. I felt my own anger rise as this young, vibrant soul related the last tragic minutes of her life on the earth, and my anger became overwhelming when she asked her mother to forgive and even *pray* for her killer—he needed our help to move closer to the Infinite Light. At this point I was white-knuckled at the injustice of it all. To me, this guy should be rotting away, and I cannot add to this mother's pain by telling her to *pray* for this scum. Without speaking aloud, I told this soul in my head, "You must be kidding—he killed *you*, and now you want to kill your mother with this sentiment?" Before I could even finish the thought, I felt the energy of the soul quickly diminish, like a brownout of electricity. The next sound I heard was not of the young woman, but what sounded like a group of souls who spoke in a hollow, yet powerful voice that filled my head. I could not see them, but I could feel their presence, and they filled my head with the sound of an impatient, perturbed tone. *"You cannot judge the words you hear,"* they admonished. *"In yourself, you are nothing. Your path is to speak for the souls. Follow that path."* The sound they made shook me out of my self-righteous attitude, right down to my foundation. The energy from the young woman re-emerged, and I continued with the session, telling the woman word for word what her daughter wanted me to relate. When the session was over, the woman thanked me. She told me that it didn't surprise her that her daughter would ask for forgiveness of someone who did her wrong—that it was so much like her daughter to think of others before herself. It helped her, she told me, to understand that her daughter was truly back to her old self again in the hereafter, and at peace with her passing. Hearing this made me all the more embarrassed at assuming I knew better than the souls communicating what their loved ones needed to hear. I thanked the woman, and showed her out, grateful she was the last appointment of the night.

I was supposed to go to devotions at the local church that night with my friends Neal and Tracy—something we did every week. My face was still hot from embarrassment and I was emotionally wiped out. I was admonished by the souls just like when I was a little boy, and the feeling brought back all the bad memories of being singled out and made to look the fool. I couldn't face going to St. Killian's and seeing the faces of the people who regularly went to vespers—those good, decent people whose faith was strong enough to accept without question whatever befell them in their lifetime. I felt like a failure, and the responsibility of speaking for the souls was something too overwhelming for me to understand. I sat on my bed and started to cry, feeling sorry for myself and anybody else who thought giving me the ability to hear the souls was a good idea. "I'm no good at this," I cried, to anyone who might be listening. "You got the *wrong* guy. I will *never* do another session." All there was around me was silence. It figures, I thought. The one time I needed the souls to talk, no one was there. My head hurt and I felt suddenly very tired, so I lay facedown on the bed, picking my head up just long enough to wipe the tears from my face. From the corner of my eye though, I caught a glimpse of light that radiated from the bedroom wall. As I focused in on that light, it radiated and became larger, and eventually took the form of a woman—a woman whose image I knew quite well. St. Frances Xavier Cabrini, called "Mother Cabrini" to those she ministered to, appeared in the light, gently smiling down at me. When she was on the earth, she was a patroness to immigrants—those who found themselves frightened and alone in a strange land. Believe me, the significance of her appearing was not lost on me—I also felt like a stranger in the land of the Souls, not understanding their language or customs, not knowing what I was doing there. *"George,"* she said plainly, but kindly. *"This is your path, the one you must follow, just like every other soul on the earth. The souls are grateful for your help, and you will never be alone—we will be with you. We cannot promise you reward in this lifetime, but we can promise it for you in the next."*

The light started to fade, as did the apparition of Mother Cabrini. *"I am in your corner,"* she said as she disappeared—something she would later say more than once in my life. It made me feel better, and her tone was so soothing. As I drifted off to sleep, only one thought remained in my head—all right, maybe I'll give this thing another chance.

3.

THE MIRACLE *of* COMMUNICATION

One of my biggest idiosyncrasies is that I have no capacity to deal with noise. Not your common, everyday noises, but those insistent, irritating ones—like car stereos booming as they pass down the street, or someone shouting to another person who stands four inches away from them. This was the reason why, in 1987, I gathered together whatever savings I had and decided to move from my tiny apartment to a real home of my own. I had started doing private sessions from my apartment for people who either knew me or knew of me by word of mouth in the community, all the while keeping my full-time job with the phone company. It was a breakneck pace—nine to five o'clock at a switchboard and then six to ten o'clock at home with clients for the sessions. When relatives or friends needed to stay a while with me, I would have to conduct the sessions in my bedroom—some of those brave, pioneer clients at the beginning actually sat on the bed listening while I sat on the floor and discerned their loved ones in the hereafter. The hectic pace of work, the cramped space, and the insufferable noise of an apartment complex with walls as thin as paper sent me out into the home buyer market ill-prepared, but enthusiastic.

I am living proof of the old adage that the Infinite Light (or God, if you prefer) watches over fools and small children. I bought the second house I saw with no research or negotiating. The house cost more money than I thought I could ever raise in ten lifetimes, but somehow I was able to manage the down payment. By anyone's standards, the house was an ordinary one on a nice street in a working-class neighborhood, but to me, it was a palace of peace and solitude in the country. I suppose if I had been less in a hurry about buying *something*, I would probably have made better choices (or cheaper ones, at least). But I was drawn to this house, not because of the backyard, or the extra bedroom, or an "eat-in" kitchen you could really eat in. In all actuality, it was the first-floor room that I was drawn to more than anything else in the house. It was, and still is today, the Quiet Room.

The Quiet Room had in it one overstuffed chair and two ugly lamps—the pole type that had its own little table built right onto it. They were parting gifts from the previous homeowners, who thought so little of them that it was easier to leave them in the room than to discard them. I accepted the furniture gladly, because there was no more money in my budget to furnish the room. The chair was also very comfy, and somehow it fit the feeling of the room. And the room did have a distinct feeling; there was a palpable energy about this room which gave it a feeling of calm. I knew immediately that this would be the room that I would do sessions in when I made the decision to leave my full-time job and devote my time to what the souls were insisting I do for years—concentrate on communicating their messages to their loved ones here. I continued to work in that room for many years, and the walls have heard many stories—some tragic, some hopeful, some disturbing, and even some funny. There have been literally thousands of people who have come and gone through that room, from here *and* hereafter, and somehow everyone has left their mark in one way or another. What I experienced in that room led to the writing of this book. The souls want to be heard. Not just individually to people one at a time, like in the sessions, but on a much wider scale—to as many people who will listen. That is the true miracle of communication with the souls in the hereafter. They want to help shape our understanding about the world around us and the world to come—the world they happily inhabit. I have found that through these messages, I am both student and teacher—I must learn, then I must teach others what I have learned.

Working in the Quiet Room was an ongoing education in mediumship. At the very beginning of my work with the souls and their loved ones here, I was much too *earthbound* in my philosophy—the tragic stories were really tough to hear, the injustice was hard to deal with, and the pain of otherwise wonderful people was hard to reconcile. What began happening as I continued sessions in that room, however, was that I was noticing how well the souls in the hereafter were taking their own passing. Their *circumstance* of death was not important to them—they reported the manner of their passing with no real concern. I also noticed that they didn't care at all what became of their bodies on the earth. In fact, they now thought of their body as the old suit they wore when they were on the earth—discarded when it was no longer needed. I began looking and listening more carefully to the souls, and what I realized startled me. They are *well*—young, pain-free, able to walk and run, to experience joy again, and truly *happy* in the hereafter. It began to dawn on me that it really is rather a happy ending in the hereafter, no matter how bad we think their passing was. It is truly a case of the end justifying the means, and it gave me much better insight and more perspective on the souls and their passing. We on the earth see our loved ones as dead, but the souls are more alive than we are. I finally started understanding that the exhilaration I felt during a session was the sheer *joy* of life the souls had in the hereafter. That concept changed forever the way I thought about the souls and my ability to hear them.

One of the most frequently asked questions of me is what it is like to communicate with the souls in the hereafter. My answer is to tell people I do not know what it is like *not* to communicate with the souls— to learn from their spirituality, their patience, their understanding, and sometimes their humor. The ability to hear and see the souls who want to communicate has been as natural to me as it is for people to see color; it is not extraordinary unless someone who cannot see color points it out. Only then does the process—seeing something someone else cannot— become extraordinary. The process of hearing or seeing the souls in the hereafter is not so much a question of "on" or "off," but rather whether I am "tuned in" or "not tuned in." The currents of electromagnetic energy that the souls use to communicate are always open, very much the same way radio waves are always in the air, regardless of whether the radio is on or not. The souls use these currents to communicate to each of us; but for some reason, my brain is able to tune into and organize their thoughts more clearly. When I hear the souls, I am very conscious and very aware on this level, but I am also conscious and aware on *their* level as well. It is very much like having a television on in the background while you are speaking on the phone. You won't hear the television unless you consciously focus yourself away from the phone to the television. It is for this very reason that I feel like I am always listening to two conversations—one on the earth, and the other in the hereafter. Even if the souls are not speaking, the line is always open. It is a constant in my life that took some getting used to, not only because I have to focus either on the souls or on the earth, but also because it makes me rather inattentive to the physical world around me. I have had many friends and coworkers laugh because they knew I did not hear a word they just told me—my mind was elsewhere, probably listening to the transmissions of the other side that I suddenly became focused on. It is like having each foot in a different world.

Even when I am not consciously focused to what the souls are telling me, they still have the ability to speak directly to my subconscious, where their messages will still be heard and noted whether I realize it consciously or not. This is the way the souls plant the seeds of hope within all of us without our realizing they have actually helped guide us. The souls want to help us without running our lives, so their suggestions whispered into our subconscious will still ring in us, whether we have actually heard them audibly or not. The only difference between myself and most people is that the souls can appeal to me directly and consciously.

Sometimes the messages from the souls are intended for others, like in a session, but sometimes the messages are told to me so that I can share them with the world about hope, peace, and fortitude during our struggles on the earth. There are some messages, however, that even I cannot understand, and they are told to me in a dream state so that I can receive the information without even being conscious of having received it. I regularly dream of St. Catherine Labouré, who sits near my bed and speaks to my subconscious. I recognize in these dreams that the information she is giving me is quite profound and life-changing, but I am at odds to produce even one bit of information when I am awake. I think perhaps that is her intention, and it is the souls' way of keeping me to a higher purpose in this lifetime without fully understanding what it is. It makes for an interesting irony—no matter how many times I hear from the souls, and no matter how many profound messages they give me, it is not for me to understand the earth and why things happen the way they do any better than anyone else who is struggling here. My relationship with the souls renders me no special treatment—I am a student here just like everyone else. I do know, however, that I have been entrusted with a special job while I am here—to give the messages of the souls in the hereafter a human voice. It is a responsibility whose importance I understand very well and take seriously, and have since the first time their words rang in my heart.

The wise words of the souls have always been in my life, at times whether I liked it or not, and guided my path here, again, whether I liked it or not. The souls are very much like concerned parents who know they must teach and protect, but also know when they must allow us to run free and stumble on our own. Each of us has a lot of learning to do, and I am no exception—the souls allow the gift of free will until all that freedom and lack of judgment sends us too far afield from where we should be. Then, without judging, they silently walk with us back to the straight road of knowing right from wrong. I know that if my emotions get the better of me in any situation and my thoughts go to the wrong way of handling it, I will be reminded in pretty short order that obedience to my spiritual journey is more important, and love stronger than hate. The souls know I am human, and prone to the same pettiness and childishness as everyone else, but they also have a job for me to do. I have to be able to communicate their messages of hope to their loved ones here, so the souls will step in when they need to, in order to ensure that I am communicating with clearness of mind and purity of heart.

THE MECHANICS OF COMMUNICATION

Although I have said this many times over the years, it bears repeating—I do not communicate with the souls, so much as *they* communicate with *me*. Their goal during a session is to reach out to their family still here on the earth, and it is something they do willingly because they care about us, and want us to know they have moved on to their reward. The souls communicate for a variety of reasons, but the most important reason by far is because they *want* to. They want to help us understand that all is not lost when physical life here is over, and that we are all on a road which will eventually take us back to them, where they are waiting for us in the grace and beauty of the hereafter. And the souls *are* waiting for us—they promise they will be there when we arrive. Forget what you might have read or hear about the "dead"—they are not resting, you will *never* be bothering them by thinking of them constantly, and asking for their help whenever you need it will *not* keep them from moving on in the hereafter. They have also told me without exception that they will help us to help ourselves here as often as they can, no matter how many times we ask them. For them it is a joy to help our spiritual growth on the earth, and they are in the hereafter working as our "guardian angels" so that we can come to the same reward in the hereafter when our time on the earth is done.

Another thing the souls have told me is that we can communicate to our loved ones on the other side whenever we want—they will always be listening. The souls have also told me that you don't need a medium for the souls to reach out to you—the souls are able to communicate to us in many ways, even if they are not as clear as what I do in the sessions. Their goal is to help us understand that we are never alone in our journey on the earth, and very often people have reported to me having dreamt about their loved ones, or smelled a fragrance that brings a strong presence of their loved one with it, or even having seen them briefly. Those who haven't had an experience of their loved one trying to reach out to them should not despair or become concerned; each of the souls has told me that when we are ready to understand and accept a sign from them, it will happen. They also caution us not to expect a "burning bush," or other obvious signs, for proof that the souls are still around us; sometimes the signs are subtle and easily missed. Regardless, the souls assure us that they are *always* around when we need them, especially at times when we feel the most alone or frightened. Part of their spiritual growth in the hereafter is to guide us through the remaining years of our lives here—a job they are most happy and willing to do, for as long as it takes before they see us again.

I am glad to see that in recent years, there has been more of an understanding of mediumship and its value as a form of grief therapy. Hearing from our loved ones is a wonderful thing, if only to get closure and to help us understand loss as a temporary separation from our loved ones. As with any field that suddenly finds itself in vogue, mediumship is also fraught with people who claim to be able to teach others how to "communicate with the dead." Although it is only my humble opinion, I do not for a second believe that mediumship can be taught, no sooner than someone can be taught to have blue eyes. There may be people who "feel" they can communicate with the souls, and even teach others to have this "feeling," but if you could be me for five minutes, you would be able to tell the difference between a "feeling" and direct communication from the souls. Something physiological changes in my brain when I am listening to the souls communicate—it is almost as if I am dreaming awake. My brain waves will register a "sleep state" while I am fully awake during a session—something that has been tested many times through analysis of my brain waves while hearing from the souls.

There is a very good reason why not everyone can hear from the souls in the hereafter, and it is the same reason why the souls will not *prove* to the world's satisfaction that they are in fact communicating to the earth. It is simply an issue of faith. Part of our existence here is to live with some circumstances that the heart must understand even though they are illogical to the mind. The souls want us to believe in our hearts that there is a reason to bring peace, joy, and love to the earth in order to find the path to the hereafter. If the existence of the hereafter was proven to us without any doubt, then working toward a spiritual perfection would be something we *had* to do, rather than something we *want* to do. Again, the choice is up to us—to believe what our hearts see rather than what our minds understand. Part of everyone's path on the earth is to keep our hope and faith in spite of tragedy and disbelief—a learning lesson that the souls there will *never* take from us. Besides, they have told me many times, we will find out for sure soon enough—when we ourselves enter the hereafter.

In the course of hearing from so many souls in the hereafter, I have found that the souls understand exactly what they are doing during a session, and will communicate the information *they* feel is necessary. They have a variety of jobs to do during a session—they try to help us understand that they do in fact exist, and they also want us to realize that they have been listening to us and following our lives since we last saw them. As much as it would make my job easier, I can no sooner *make* the souls tell their loved ones here what they want to hear during the session than I can make things work to my own satisfaction. It is up to the souls what they want to communicate. They do, however, know that we have a need to hear from one soul more than another, and they seem to also have the ability to answer the questions we have in our hearts, without our having to actually ask out loud. It is one of the most fascinating aspects of the sessions, and the reason why I don't allow the sitter during a session to ask anything. If the souls are able to communicate, *then they should also know who you need to hear from and why.* I cannot stress that strongly enough. While I understand that they cannot answer everything for us, they will do their best to help us understand that they are looking out for us and are still with us.

I tend to caution people before a session that the souls will not perform "parlor tricks" for their family—in essence, proving beyond a shadow of a doubt that it is, in fact, them communicating—but I do notice in some of the sessions that the souls will go out of their way to help us understand the value of their appearing for us when our hope needs to be bolstered. It often happens to me that I am visited by a soul, sometimes days or even weeks before their loved ones on earth will meet me. Their express purpose is to impress upon me to bring something with me to the session that is intended to help their loved ones here know for sure they have made communication. Sometimes it can be as simple as a prayer card, and other times they will be insistent that I bring an object of their choosing to the session. A while back, I was asked by a television program to allow them to film a session with a family. A few days before the taping, I was visited by a soul of a young man who insisted I bring a stuffed toy frog with me to the taping. So out we went, two days before flying to Cleveland, to find a gift shop that sells frogs. We walked through the mall, but all we could find were the usual teddy bears and dolls. *No,* the soul insisted—it *must* be a frog. Our last chance was a card store at the end of the mall. There we found what the soul asked for—one green stuffed frog. I packed it in my bag and took it with me to Cleveland. During the taped session with a lovely couple who had lost their son in an automobile accident, this soul made reference again to the frog. I told the couple that their son had impressed upon me to bring them the frog because it had significant meaning to them. They accepted it with a look of complete surprise and gratitude, indicating that, indeed, it had significance to them. It was only afterward that the couple told me that their son's nickname for his father was "The Frog." For some reason, it was important enough for the soul of that young man to appeal to me a few days in advance to bring proof that he was really communicating and was alive in the hereafter—something that his parents may have been struggling to understand. I wish the souls would do this for every family, but they don't. By the same token, not every family needs to be convinced in the same way that their loved ones are communicating to them for sure. It seems that the souls know better than I do what is the best way to appeal to their family—something I will always be grateful to them for. In their own way—through the use of a certain phrase, a name, a circumstance, or even a physical prop, the souls are able to impress upon their families that they are really hearing from them.

Sometimes, however, no matter what the souls do to help us understand, their words fall on deaf ears. I had a mother and adult son come to see me, and during the session a young man appeared, telling me he was *son* and *brother* to the couple in front of me. Although he communicated about the circumstance of his passing, and gave information about the lives of his mom and brother, I could still see the look of skepticism and denial in his brother's face. Near the end of the session, the brother blurted out, "What is his name?" I waited for the answer, and his brother in the hereafter set about the process of explaining to me that his name was Daniel. His brother, nonplussed by this information, told me, "That's not what *I* called him—what does he tell you I called him?" I wondered whether this young soul was going to bother trying to convince his brother that he was really communicating, but he did, surprising even me. He showed me a cup of Dannon yogurt, and told me to drop the last letter. "He tells me it's Danno," I told his brother. I could see that the information surprised the gentleman, but he did not relent in his disbelief. He left the session in a huff—more disturbed by the information than comforted. Even the souls will concede that they can only walk us to the river of understanding, but they cannot make us drink. Sometimes skepticism is borne more out of fear than disbelief— it might open up avenues that we are not ready to deal with. The souls are remarkably philosophical about this, however—they simply say, "Each will understand in his own time."

One of the wonderful things about my relationship with the souls in the hereafter is the humanity that comes in dealing with people on such a personal level. I have made some great friends, and I feel as though sometimes the sessions are as much for me to learn something as they are for the families attending. Sometimes I am moved by the pain of a family who must endure tragedy, and also will search for the lesson in their pain. Other times, however, in the middle of tragic circumstances come small moments of laughter, whether accidental or intended. This light in the midst of sadness is a gift from our loved ones that cannot be measured.

Not too long ago, I had a session with two lovely young women with a distinct *Noo Yawk* accent, who, as it was discovered in the session, were sisters. In the course of the session, their mother appeared and talked at length about having breast cancer, and having done all she could to survive long enough to see her daughters become young women. It was an emotional session—their mom spoke about having to put on a brave face and keep life as normal as possible in order not to frighten her daughters while she went through the battery of tests and treatments. In the end, she told me, she realized that this was the completion of her road on the earth, and now, she is trying to help her daughters not to be needlessly frightened about their own futures. I could tell that the sisters were having trouble coping with the information they were hearing, and at some points I would stop speaking and allow the sobbing to subside before moving on. I began to worry that the communication was going to be too much for them to handle. But the women tried hard to keep themselves together, and listened the best they could through their tears.

"Your mom tells me that she couldn't initially accept her diagnosis . . ." I told them.

"Yeah . . . that's true," they answered, crying.

". . . and she had a very rough time prior to her passing," I continued.

"Uh-huh," they both answered, wiping away tears.

"Your mom also tells me she fought it."

"*What??*" The women looked at each other, and then to me, suddenly surprised.

"Your mom says she fought it," I repeated, assuming they did not hear me.

The sisters looked at me, then at each other, and burst out laughing.

I was stunned by the sudden laughter. "What's so funny?" I asked them, slightly aghast at the inappropriate response to the message.

"What did you say? My mother *farted?*"

"No, dear," I said as carefully as I could. *"FOUGHT IT."*

"*Ohhh*—okay," they giggled.

I have to admit that after that "misunderstanding," the session had a decidedly lighter feeling for the sisters, and thinking about it on my drive home later on, I laughed so hard I had to pull over for a few minutes. Although I still smile when I think of that session, I marvel at how the souls can help lighten the mood by creating a little humor in an otherwise tragic situation. I don't believe for a second that any of it was accidental, after seeing how their pain was diffused, if only for a little while. The souls, once again, may manipulate things (or words) just a little bit to help lighten our load and nudge us, even giggling, back on the road to hope.

THE REALITY OF COMMUNICATION— FOR BETTER OR WORSE

Mediumship is a wonderful opportunity to hear more clearly the wisdom of our loved ones in the hereafter, and that information can have a profound and life-changing effect on how we look at our world and the world of the souls. The one thing mediumship *cannot do*, however, is bring our loved ones back. I know that sounds rather simplistic, and something everyone knows, but it does bear repeating. Very often we will get very frantic calls to the office from someone who has just lost a loved one. The calls are heartbreaking. In the hours and few days after a loved one has passed, we will all scramble for a way to understand and cope, but some people just can't accept the passing and think if they could just communicate with their loved one, somehow they would stay alive. They tell me that what they want is a session—to hear that their loved ones are all right and at peace, but I know from my experience that what they really want is to postpone the inevitable pain of the grief process. But no amount of communication with the souls will bring them back to us in the physical form. It is up to us now to accept the passing, and there is no short-circuiting the process of grief. The only thing that saves us from complete despair is time and perspective. In time, the pain will be easier to bear, and we will be able to survive the grief—one more minute, one more hour, one more day, one more week. The souls caution us, however, that in this instance, we cannot rely on them to pull us through it—they can only assist us in our slow walk back to our senses.

Communication with the souls is also not a panacea for all our mangled hopes and misunderstandings about life, death, and the world around us. Many people have come to a session expecting that the souls will sort the pieces of our lives and put them into tidy order for us. They will not. The souls tell us that no matter how much they want to, they cannot live our lives for us and make the road any easier. We will still have to make our own choices and learn from our experiences the way we choose to. One time a woman, her two adult sons, and one adult daughter came to a session, and the woman's husband (and the children's father) spoke at length about the strife that had consumed the family since his passing. He even joked that he was glad he was no longer on the earth to have to deal with it. He let them know as best he could how much he loved them all, and while he was concerned about the lack of communication between siblings and mother, he knew that in time they would learn to focus more on what was important—the family. The bottom line, he told them, was to "not sweat the small stuff" and to value their relationships with each other more than trinkets and money. As the session came to an end, I looked up to find the family completely underwhelmed by the messages. "Well, I thank you for your time," the woman said curtly as she stood up. "But I have a hard time believing that my husband would have *nothing* to say about who should get the house and who should get his watch. *Ask* him who they were supposed to go to." Before I could even answer her, I heard her husband laughing in the hereafter, saying, *"Tell her it's her battle—I'm done."* I told her what her husband said, and one of her sons laughed. "That's Daddy," he said. The message had no effect on her attitude; she smiled tightly and left as her children said good-bye to me. I couldn't help feeling a little annoyed later on. I don't expect everyone to feel like the sessions were an earth-shattering experience, but this woman sat through an entire session where her husband poured his heart out for his family, and the session was a failure in her mind because he did not conduct the session the way *she* thought it should go. As much as I know I have no control over what the souls will and will not talk about (free will cannot be changed, here or hereafter), it still bothered me that the souls do so much to help us understand what is really important, and we just brush it aside to hear about trivial matters. I wish I could be like the souls, who laugh and take it all in stride—but I guess that is part of what I need to learn here.

The question I am most frequently asked, especially by media, is how I feel about skeptics. How should I feel? We should all be skeptics of something we cannot see, feel, or understand. We will never really know for sure about the Garden of Souls until we find ourselves there. I only know what I have heard, seen, and felt from the souls in the hereafter, and although I can share this information, unless someone can be me for five minutes, it is very difficult to understand. It is impossible to believe something just because someone tells you. You have to *feel* it. What I've found, however, is that when people experience loss, suddenly, whether it is conscious or not, they desperately *need* to understand more about the souls and the hereafter. I do believe that it is one of the profound phenomena we experience when we are dealing with the loss of a loved one. I'm not so sure this need to understand is something that we come upon ourselves; I think it is something given to us by our loved ones in the hereafter to help us understand. Some people go their whole lives without being the least bit interested in a foreign country, until they know someone who has recently moved there. Then the need to understand another culture begins to creep into the thought process. It is very much the same when our loved ones move on to the hereafter— they have simply moved to another place.

I have found, however, that there are two kinds of skeptics—those who say, "I don't know," and those who say, "I don't *want* to know." I have to admit that the latter is the more difficult to deal with. I still meet people who think what I do is a bunch of bunk. They are entitled to their opinion, for a variety of reasons. First, many skeptics come to their opinions out of fear—fear of the prospect of accountability for our actions on the earth once our time here is done, and fear that their religion or philosophical understanding may not allow them the latitude to consider the possibility of communication with those whom they consider "dead." This is always surprising to me, considering that almost all religions believe in life hereafter, and that their deities have spoken to the earth at various times throughout history. I watched in amazement a few years ago the great Dr. Elisabeth Kubler-Ross, considered the "mother" of all death and dying issues, handle herself during an interview with a Christian fundamentalist. This very educated member of the clergy told Elisabeth that belief in mediumship was "the devil's work on earth," and that nobody could communicate with the "dead."

"You are a Christian, aren't you?" Elisabeth asked him, through her halting Swiss accent.

"Of course," he responded.

"And you pray to Jesus Christ, do you not?"

"Certainly, every day."

"And he hears your prayers, yes?"

"Every one."

"Then, my friend," she said wryly, "*you* are communicating with the dead."

As I mentioned, there are people who I know well who thought what I do is nonsense—that is their right. They thought that way right up until the time their loved ones communicated to them. I must say that when the souls want to make the case for belief in them, they tend to pull out all the good silverware. My friend Marta recently married a gentleman named Larry, who avoided the subject of mediumship every time we saw each other. While he never said anything directly to me about his disbelief, he did make it known to Marta that he had no interest in my work. But when Marta needed to hear the communication from her twin sister who passed on recently, he stood by her and accompanied her to the session. During the session, Marta's sister spoke at length about her illness and how glad she was to find herself in good health and truly happy on the other side, continuing her work with children. Marta's husband did his very best to feign polite interest. At one point, though, near the end of the session, Marta's sister announced to me, "*Michael is here.*" I looked to Marta with the information, but her sister told me, "*No, not to her. To him—tell him Michael is here.*" I turned to Marta's husband and repeated what the soul said. There was a look of disbelief on his face. The next voice to communicate was a young male, telling me that he is related to Larry, a cousin, who passed on young.

"Yes," Larry answered, visibly stunned.

"He tells me he fell from great height, and passes on young."

"Yes."

"I don't know what he means," I continued. "He says nobody knows him?"

"Yes," Larry said, sheepishly.

Michael continued to communicate about his passing having a profound effect on Larry's fear of death, but went on to explain that he is around Larry like a guardian angel, and that he was proud of Larry's accomplishments. He ended the session by saying that Larry owed Marta one, for making it possible for him to communicate to Larry.

After the session ended, Larry was pale. Marta asked him why he had never mentioned having a cousin who was killed at an early age. Larry could only respond by telling her that he knew when they were dating that Marta knew me, and that if I was really able to "talk to the dead," that his cousin Michael would find a way to get to him. Larry apologized to me, but there was nothing to apologize for. I told him how the souls had reminded me on many occasions, "Each in his own time." But I must admit that the souls do love setting the disbelievers on their ears once in a while.

The only exception I will ever take when it comes to skeptics is when those who "know better" decide that it is up to them to champion the cause of the "poor, lowly bereaved" who are being "duped" into believing that communication with their deceased loved ones is possible. The most insidious of the "skeptic police," who tout themselves as "scientific experts," feel they must "protect" the bereaved because they feel the bereaved are not in a correct frame of mind to understand that they are being "taken advantage of." I have said many times that because I have held myself out as a medium and stand behind my work, I have no problem being the target of naysayers and skeptics. They can say what they want about my ability and are certainly entitled to their opinions. What I will never allow is attacks against the bereaved for their spiritual beliefs. I have never seen someone lose their capacity to reason or make qualified value judgments just because they lost a loved one. Being bereaved does not make someone stupid—just bereaved. It is amazing to me when I hear that even members of the bereaved person's family will fight with them tooth and nail not to believe in the existence of mediumship, at the very time they should be understanding and eager to help—even if that means honoring a different way of thinking. I have found that my clients, nearly all of them in bereaved circumstances, have done their homework with regard to mediumship, and are quite savvy, when it comes to placing their trust and hope in communication with their loved ones in the hereafter.

As with everything on the earth, time will tell. I have heard in many sessions the souls telling their loved ones here, *"There is a hereafter, and you will soon see it—one of us will be proven wrong, and it won't be us. When it is your time to graduate from the earth, you will never be so glad you were wrong."* The souls understand we are working under a severe lack of information, and they applaud our faith and hope in spite of it. I have had sessions where a soul would tell me, *"When I was on the earth, I thought this was a lot of hooey. Boy, was*

I glad it isn't." What I find most interesting is that those who were the most opposed to the idea of communication with the hereafter actually make the most active communicators from the hereafter. They will do what they can to help those who are frightened by the prospect of life hereafter to have an easier transition to this understanding, whether it happens here or there. Like the souls say, each in his own time.

Communication with the souls truly is a miracle—of hope, of love, and of understanding. The souls have told me that nothing we endure on the earth will be too much for us to bear, and that no experience where we learn to be better people is ever wasted. I know in my lifetime of listening to the souls that the communication will never be perfect or understood by everyone. But the souls remind me that no matter how deaf we become to the wise words of the hereafter, they will never stop trying to send messages of hope to the earth.

4.

LIFE *in the* GARDEN—THE SOULS WANT *to* TELL YOU

Once or even twice in your lifetime, if you are very lucky, you will be treated to a moment of such clarity that it will bring new meaning to the very purpose of your life. It is the moment in our lives we can call the Big Picture, or what I like to call, The Understanding—the point in our lives when things finally start making sense. It can happen at any time in our lives, but with some luck and a lot of life experience, it happens sooner rather than later. We on the earth tend to walk blindly through major portions of our life until something or *someone* reaches into us, and, like a magic trick, produces a beautiful bouquet of understanding where none had been. The Understanding does not have to be anything particularly groundbreaking or new—it just has to be something, perhaps insignificant in itself, but has the power to push open a door in our consciousness that otherwise could not have been pried open previously. Once opened, however, it can flood every room of our being with rivers of knowledge and mountains of self-awareness where only the flat, dry land of complacence stood. A few years back, about twenty years into my work as a medium, I had one such moment of clarity that unexpectedly gave me real insight into the purpose and meaning of many events that have shaped my life and work so far.

As I saw it then, my job in the course of a session was only to provide an opportunity for the souls in the hereafter to use me as their conduit to their loved ones here. To me, the ability to communicate with the souls in the hereafter was a type of service I provided, mainly because I was able to, much in the same way I connected calls as an operator for the telephone company. And in both instances, my responsibility was to make the connection to the best of my ability, not to participate in the call. I heard the messages and repeated them to the loved ones here, but did my best not to "listen in." I had learned long ago that it was in my best interest to stay out of the discernment; I had to remove myself emotionally, because it was the only way I could ensure that my feelings wouldn't interfere with, and subsequently bias the communication. I assumed, though, that because I was not directly related to the principals of the session, the messages were not intended to make any difference in my life anyway. So, during a session I would listen to the information communicated to me by the souls, and I would repeat the messages as best I could, without really listening further than the actual words, phrases, or messages. Then, without notice, something out of the ordinary happened to make me understand that there was a lot more in the messages that the souls had in mind.

I usually don't remember what messages are relayed during a session, and sometimes never get to understand why a particular message holds such meaning to the family hearing it (unless the family tells me afterward). I am usually told by the souls that the specific messages are meant to appeal to something deep within the hearts of the family, and it is not necessarily important that I understand. That is what I was *usually* told. All of that seemed to change, however, when the parents of an eight-year-old girl named Elizabeth came to see me. Elizabeth was killed in a fall from a tree outside her family's farm in Lancaster, Pennsylvania. Her parents both felt that if they had only been more vigilant about watching her that day, or never taught her how to climb a tree, that the tragedy would never have happened. During the session, Elizabeth spoke to her parents, trying to help save their sanity by assuring them she was in a safe, happy place, and that it truly was her time to continue in the hereafter. Her goal in communicating, it seemed to me, was to help diffuse some of the anger and profound guilt her parents felt. It came up several times in the session that the parents blamed each other, at least secretly, for contributing to Elizabeth's passing, and it was all Elizabeth could do to help them understand that the passing was no one's fault. To get her message across, Elizabeth reached into my own memory and produced a scene from a movie I knew well, so that I would instantly know the point she was driving at. The souls seem to have any information I have in *my* head at their disposal, and they will use it when they need to. This is something many souls have been able to do because it seems to save time, and it ensures that I can understand the meaning of their message so that I can report it more accurately. It is like the old adage of a picture being worth a thousand words. In this case, the young girl showed me a scene from the movie *The Wizard of Oz*—near the end, when Dorothy is told that the power to return to Kansas was always within her, but she had to find it out for herself. Before Dorothy could do that, however, she was presented with the task of fighting destructive elements along her way, and helping others to find what was already within them also. It is a poignant scene and a metaphor of sorts, intended to teach all of us to look within ourselves for the strength we need to continue on our own "brick road." I understood immediately the point Elizabeth was trying to make; she wanted her mother and father to find the strength within themselves to help each other through their worst nightmare as parents. I was glad that Elizabeth "found" that movie in my memory because nothing I can think of could have illustrated that point better. I listened, watched, and then responded, telling her parents what she showed me and what she hoped they would understand from it.

Ordinarily, that small scene would not be the stuff of which a catharsis is made, but this session moved from the ordinary to the extraordinary when young Elizabeth flashed the scene in my head again. At first, I didn't understand what she was doing—she had already shown me the scene, and the message was already relayed to her parents. But as I looked again in my mind, it was as if she were holding that scene up to me—like a mirror to my own life. The scene now stirred up memories of the times in my life when I needed to look within for strength and battle my own fears in order to be able to help others on their road here. All at once I understood by this simple act that the messages from the souls are directly related to our ability to hold them to our own lives, like a mirror, where they will take on new and dramatic meaning.

After this meeting, I came to a much broader understanding of what the souls are trying to teach us. Not only are the souls' messages for each of us specific to their relationship to us, but every message from the hereafter is intended to educate and create hope in *anyone* who can hear it. The souls were not just communicating *through* me, they were also communicating *to* me. Their intent was to have *me* understand and benefit from the

messages of comfort and hope just as much as their loved ones specifically. The souls understand full well that their communication can reach
a much broader audience than just the people sitting in a session, and
that their messages will have a real and quantifiable benefit to anyone
who will listen to their wisdom. They have accomplished their struggles
on the earth, and now feel honor bound to give something back to the
earth when they communicate. Their hope is that if they cannot make
our struggles here easier, at least they can help us understand why they
are so necessary. It was a pivotal point in my understanding of just how
much the souls are capable of in the hereafter, and why it is so important for them to communicate. They are not just communicating to
their loved ones here—they are communicating to the *earth*.

After my realization, I tried to listen much more closely to the messages in the session and noticed how patient the souls were in communicating the information about our world and theirs. They want us to
listen and learn, but only when we are able to understand and accept
what they are telling us. Although I always knew that what the souls were
trying to tell us was important, I needed to understand that the messages
can apply to everyone's life. The souls' first project was to re-educate me
and make me a better listener. There is no reason why my leap into self-
awareness and understanding should have taken so long, but I admit that
I am stubborn and did not want my own belief system to be dismantled.
Just like everyone else, I had my own ideas about how my life should proceed, and my own system of values already in place. What the souls
started saying sometimes ran contrary to everything I was taught, but I
came to find that their vision is so much farther reaching than ours
could ever be. I must say, though, that for the souls to make me understand, it was certainly an uphill battle for them. Many times the impact
of the messages from the hereafter had fallen limp at my feet, because I

heard the words but could not hear the *message*. I know that human emotions like anger, resentment, jealousy, and hatred get in the way of hearing that message, but part of our challenge is to find it within ourselves to re-open our hearts and minds, especially after tragedy, to really hear their words. The souls want to share their messages—they want to *tell* you. They have set about making that happen in a variety of ways. Slowly but surely the souls are able to shake us loose from our flawed, narrow beliefs about life, and teach us about creating heaven on earth for ourselves, others, and this planet of all creatures and things. Like every other circumstance where their help is needed, the souls in the hereafter are willing to speak to us, even if we are not willing or even *able* to listen. They know there will come a time when we all will hear them. It is the reason why they asked that this book be written—to share what I know about the beauty of their world, and the ability we all possess to create beauty on the earth. We can only imagine a life free of emotional and physical pain. The souls understand that we on the earth are bombarded with images and accounts of those, still earthbound, who want to tell us about a world they do not know; but the souls are the only ones who can speak with any authenticity about their existence, and it is only through them that *I* have any information at all. None of this information is my musing about what *might* await us in the hereafter; the information comes strictly from the souls, through thousands of sessions, and also through their directly relating to me the information they need the earth to know. I wish I could take credit for some of the wonderful things that the souls have told their loved ones through the course of a session, but I know I cannot. What the souls tell us is not so much to clearly mark the path here, but rather to focus it enough so we can see the road a little more easily, and make the journey here more meaningful and productive.

THERE LIVES A GARDEN OF SOULS

The souls have not always used the metaphor of a "Garden of Souls" to describe the hereafter. In fact, a "garden" wasn't something I could really relate to in my own life. I never paid much attention to gardens in the past, and never really understood the passion of true gardeners when they spoke in mystical terms about the "life" of their gardens. I had no interest in landscaping, no particular fascination with flowers, and to me, gardening was digging a hole, dropping a plant into that hole, and hoping for the best. I would have never come to the realization of our spiritual life as a garden, unless I was guided there by the wisdom of the souls in the hereafter. But knowledge is equal to awakening, and the souls began to toss circumstances in my path to help illustrate what would eventually become their way of referencing life on earth to life in the hereafter. I have found out that yet again, the souls know what they are doing. To liken spiritual life to a garden is to explain, in the simplest terms possible, the complex, fragile, and often wondrous nature of life here *and* hereafter.

No matter how lumbering the Philistine in you is, you cannot help but be awed by the sheer skill and beauty in Belgian gardens. Gardening is serious business there, and I remember watching the gardeners from a hotel window in Brussels as they worked in a public garden, pruning, clipping, and shaping the trees, flowers and shrubs into perfect shapes. I was struck by the degree of mastery it took to manipulate growing objects into soft sculpture, and the time and patience involved in creating this fusion of science and art. Watching the gardeners work in earnest to produce such fine results, I began to understand why the souls tell us over and over that our spirituality, like a garden, must be tended carefully. We need space and circumstance to grow, we need to be nurtured, and the process takes time and patience to see true results. If we are left without direction, we will grow into a tangled mess and eventually diminish under our own recklessness, yet if we follow the examples carefully planned for us, it is possible to grow into perfect specimens of love. We are like the beautiful plants that grow in a well-cared-for garden—we suffer from the bitter cold winds of tragic circumstance, we wither from neglect, but from the smallest amount of light and nourishment we can grow again from the dirt and become a thing of beauty. This is the answer to one of life's greatest questions; our purpose is to grow into shining examples of the Infinite Light on the earth, as well as inspire those around us with the beauty of our full-grown potential. And all of this will happen over and over, in many circumstances, through the seasons of our life here on earth.

I have a dear friend who bought a tiny house with a rather large expanse of land. Although the house needed work, his first instinct was to begin a garden right away. Armed with more enthusiasm than experience, I watched as he tore into the land, tilled the earth, and eventually began planting what he hoped to be a replica of a fine English garden. At first, the garden showed great promise, although it was hard to visualize from the tiny cuttings and sprigs what the garden would look like once the plants grew into maturity. Still, when I visited him, his enthusiasm about what the garden *would be* when it matured was enough for anyone to overlook the obvious gaps and spaces in the beds.

Fall came, then winter, and we would go out onto the deck, where he would point out the roses that will grow to profusion over there, where the shrubs will blend to form perfect boxes and lanes in the ground, and where the ivy will creep along the fence and over the arbor. Try as I could to see the beautiful garden he had in his head as he looked across the yard, all I could see was a barren plot, covered with the cold snow.

Springtime came, and when I visited, I could begin to see what he meant by the plants and colors that started bursting from the ground. In a little time, the garden would be the perfect vision he drew in his head—lush, vibrant, and awash with colors.

But things started going wrong. The plant that was supposed to be red became a garish orange, and grew so wildly it blocked out everything behind it. The rosebushes didn't even bother to grow—they remained withered sticks in the earth. The ivy made a half-hearted attempt across the bed, but quit before it climbed the arbor. Some of the boxwood died, making the lanes look like a mouth with missing teeth. What was planted with so much promise was not even a shade of what it was supposed to be. It would have been hilariously funny to me if I didn't feel so bad about his disappointment. His vision of a perfect garden disappeared into the reality of a badly grown mess of unruly plants and weedy flowers.

Disappointed, but undaunted, he regrouped and learned from his mistakes. The wild orange plant was moved to the back, where it could flourish without blocking something else. The ivy could be trained to make the perilous climb over the arbor. The roses needed more sun to survive, and the shrubs needed more water. Piece by piece, plant by plant, the garden was changed, moved, manipulated with eager hands and newfound knowledge. Now his zest for instant gratification gave way to more patience, allowing the garden to mature at its own pace and in its own time. As I visited from time to time, I began to see the many changes that both he and nature created as the garden slowly became a living fixture in his yard.

I stopped by recently to see my friend. He is in the process of selling his house. Although we were approaching fall, the weather was still warm enough to go outside to visit the garden. As I opened the gate, I was stopped in my tracks by what I saw. I stood in a perfect garden, a

beautiful rendition of one of those fine English gardens found in magazines. Roses toppled over trimly manicured shrubs. Lush plants lined
the path to ivy-covered arbors surrounded by perfectly mounded flowers of every hue. Wherever you looked, the garden was awash with color
and fragrance. It was a moving experience for me to think back and remember this sad little garden in its infancy, with its problems and bare
patches, which time and patience guided into a work of art. He created
a little piece of heaven right there, in his backyard.

It actually bothered me to think that soon all of his hard work
would be left to the inexperienced hands of someone else when he sold
his house, and that all the work he did for so long would just be left behind. I asked him if it would be hard to leave such a beautiful garden,
after so much time and effort, after so much disappointment, and after
so much triumph. "Not at all," he told me. "I'll just do it all again,
somewhere else. The reward is not so much the garden, it's having created it."

Throughout my ride home, I could not shake my friend's words
from my head. It seemed like such a waste to me to invest so much time
and energy in something, and then to walk away just when the fruits of
such hard labor could finally be enjoyed. As I drove, I felt a presence near
me—a soul I could not identify, but a comforting presence nonetheless.
I couldn't see the soul, but the soul began speaking, and its words rang
in my head—*"The soul will create many gardens on earth until it walks to the Garden of the Infinite Light."*

Talk about your "lightbulb" moments. It seemed as if, in one simple statement, every second of my work with the souls in the hereafter
and people here had become perfectly clear to me. We all come to the
earth with a perfect garden in our heads, then try and fail to reproduce
it. Circumstance may destroy many parts of it, but we continue on in
the garden of our lives, until it reaches a point when experience, hard

lessons, and patience come together to produce the garden we want. And when we are done, we walk away—back to the perfect garden we once saw. It is not even necessary to look back, because we know a better garden awaits. In this simple analogy, the souls can explain our spiritual life from here to hereafter, and the true beauty that awaits us when our work is done.

THE PROMISE OF A PERFECT GARDEN

Each of us might experience a glimmer of the world hereafter while we are on the earth, through an unexpected, happy moment, a sign of hope, or even a brief feeling of complete contentment of mind and heart. Moments are given to us on the earth, though in maddeningly small doses, by the souls and the Infinite Light to illustrate just how much we have to look forward to after our long struggle on the earth. The first blush of true love, a child's laughter, a single snowflake, the moment of true understanding—these moments are given to us, like snapshots of lovely, idyllic locales, to help us in some small way imagine the magnitude of perfection and beauty that exists in the hereafter. But the souls have told me that not even these extraordinary examples of happiness can compare with the absolute joy and peace the souls experience, once their journey on the earth is completed.

Early on in my work listening to the souls in the hereafter, I tried my best to push the limits of my consciousness to move closer to the souls that were communicating. They would come, surrounded in such profound peace and love that I found it an irresistible force—like a moth to a flame. Even briefly during the session, I could feel such energy and uncompromising love radiating from the souls, that I found myself changed in mind and spirit. The only problem was that after the souls had gone, the reality of life here would return, and I would find myself less able to tolerate the almost overwhelming disappointment and frustration that seems to envelope the earth. It always reminded me of an old adage, *"How can you keep 'em down on the farm, after they've seen Paree."* The more I saw "Paree," the less I could endure "the farm." I suspect that this is yet another of my struggles to work through while I am on the earth. At least the experience of glimpsing into their world has given me one thing: I can tell people, with all my heart and soul, that no matter how bad things look here, it will all have been worth every second.

THE TRANSITION

The souls have told me that at the moment of our passing, we shed whatever held us physically to the earth; our fear, anger, troubles, and concerns—they are all left here in the same heap as the skin, hair, and bones we carried through this existence. None of it is needed. Many have talked about the profound feeling of relief as every weight that bound them lifted away, to reveal the beautiful soul that was waiting a lifetime to break free. As souls, we are now able to move with incredible lightness toward those who have been waiting for us—loved ones, friends, and even those we didn't realize were walking silently with us through our experiences on the earth. It is a reunion, but also a monumental time in the rebirth of the soul. This is the time when the soul can take a magical look toward the earth, seeing it for the first time in perfect understanding—the needless pain, the necessary struggle, and the true beauty of those we love so much. So many of the souls have stated that they thought it would be hard to say good-bye to the earth and see the faces of pain on our loved ones left behind, but they say that as soon as they passed they understood instantly how much closer they can be to their loved ones than they could have ever been on the earth. Now, for the first time in a long time, the soul is perfect and beautiful. They are no longer ravaged by time, illness, hunger, violence, and despair—they are now as perfect as the day they came to the earth.

In the hereafter, the souls come to understand what was their mission on the earth, and how closely they were able to stay to their purpose. They are shown the movie of their lifetime—the good, the bad, the opportunities taken and the opportunities squandered. It is interesting that the souls say we here can all remember in vivid detail all the terrible things we have done during the course of our lives, but we never seem to remember the truly wonderful things we did for others, or how much we impacted another's life with our kindness. All of it, however, has been chronicled for us to review when we return to the hereafter. We are the sole judge of our performance on the earth, and we alone decide how well we had used the opportunity to grow spiritually. If the soul made good use of the opportunities to grow spiritually on the earth, the soul can progress to a higher level of spiritual understanding and light in the hereafter. If the time on the earth was wasted in evil and recklessness, the soul begins to understand for the first time how wrong their actions on the earth were, and how antithetical these actions were to their progress on the earth. With the newly found understanding, a little shame, but a heart full of true remorse, the soul places itself on a level further from the light, where lessons can be relearned and a troubled existence can be repaired. The road to the Infinite Light and reconciliation is always open for the souls who want to continue forward, and *nothing* that happened on the earth is beyond the understanding and forgiveness of the Infinite Light. The souls, together, help each other to achieve spiritual perfection in their new home.

In a perfect existence, in an endless summer day, there lives a garden of souls. The souls create a garden of their own making—whatever is pleasing to them, and whatever will bring them joy and peace. Those who went hungry on the earth find themselves surrounded by great abundance, those who never knew true happiness find themselves in the arms of acceptance and love, and those whose inner turmoil shattered their hope on the earth find themselves enveloped by peace and true understanding. Many of the souls who craved things they could never find on the earth discover these very things waiting for them in their Garden, and the souls are fed until the need to have these things are no longer important. The souls find that nothing material is necessary to their existence and spiritual growth, and they set about reaping the love and energy in their continuing journey closer to the Infinite Light. As the souls continue to learn and grow in the comfort and peace of the hereafter, they set about the work that will bring them joy—some in service to other souls, and some in service to us still on the earth. The souls now find that they are never further from us than our own thoughts, and as they are needed by us they are with us, to help us take full advantage of the opportunities to grow on the earth. Although we can continue to grow in the peace and beauty of the hereafter, the souls understand that our greatest opportunity to grow spiritually is on the earth, where the lessons are much harder, but the reward for our accomplishments is much greater.

Many of the souls in the hereafter will refer to the glory of their new world as the "vacation they never got on the earth." It is, perhaps, a gigantic understatement, but the only way they can give us the feeling of their new life in the hereafter. Their *vacation* is the absence of cares and worries, where nothing is expected unless the souls want to accomplish something, and where the pace is dictated by the soul's willingness to rest or proceed. We are in complete control of our destiny in the hereafter. The one thing I find fascinating about the existence of the souls in the hereafter is that it is ever-changing. As the souls grow in wisdom and understand the spiritual value of life in the hereafter, their value system changes. The parents of a young man I knew well on the earth came to see me very shortly after their son, Patrick, passed on from cancer at twenty-two years old. They were devastated by the loss of their son, but also very angry that he never had a chance to experience the joy of youth—falling in love, starting a career, and racing the cars he enjoyed building. During the session, Patrick gave me the feeling that he was a "kid in a candy store," proudly displaying for me the fleet of cars he could only have dreamed of on the earth. "These are *mine*," he beamed, hoping to illustrate to his parents how life, and dreams, truly continue in the hereafter. Right now, this was his version of "heaven"—having the things he cherished on the earth. Subsequently, I had an opportunity to see the parents again at a fund-raiser for cancer research about a year after their session. As I stood to say hello to them, their son Patrick appeared behind them. To me, he looked the same, but there was a new serenity about him—a kind of wisdom that made him seem more mature. He flashed into my head a scene which I have seen many times in the course of sessions with parents who have lost children—the magnificent playground in the hereafter, where children who pass on not knowing any of their relatives go to play with other children, in order to make their transition to the hereafter more normal and comforting to them. In this scene, Patrick showed me his work there—he is now a kind of "camp counselor" who takes the role of "Uncle Patrick" to give the children a feeling of safety and love once they have crossed over. He told me, "*This is what I love now.*" His parents were profoundly moved by the information he related through me, and they told me they often wondered about what he would become here, had he not passed on. The reassurance from Patrick that he has continued his life in the hereafter goes a long way in helping all of us understand that it is continuation, not termination, in the hereafter. Life does indeed go on for our loved ones in the hereafter, and it is a life of our choosing. On the earth, very often we are not afforded the choices of our life plan, but we certainly choose what is to be our life's work in the hereafter. It is one of the most satisfying things in my life to know that *choice* is one of the most beautiful gifts we will receive when we enter the Garden of Souls.

FOR EVERYTHING, THERE IS A REASON

No matter how many messages I hear from the souls in the hereafter, I find that I am no better prepared for life here than anybody else. Knowing what the souls say about why things happen on the earth does not give me a "leg up" on things here; it is still up to me, as it is for everyone else, to reconcile what I can't understand and go on faith. In this regard, we are all in the same boat—we are all struggling and learning here. I get no "special treatment." Although I do hear from the souls and understand the value of their messages, I am also human, and on my own spiritual journey here. And as much as I know about the beauty of life on the Other Side, there is much that I cannot know until my journey here is done. It is also in my life plan—as it is in everyone else's—to reconcile in my head and heart the one message from the souls that resounds more than any others: *for everything, there is a reason.*

One of the things that I have learned through listening to the souls is that all prayer is answered—but sometimes the answer to our prayer is *no*. One time in my life, I prayed to St. Theresa for something I thought I wanted more than life itself, and it didn't happen. I prayed harder. It still didn't happen. Frustrated and angry, I yelled at the portrait of her I have in my home. "Look, Lady," I spouted, "I've done everything you guys have asked me to do. I work until I'm half dead communicating messages, and all I ask is a small thing that would make my life so much happier. Is that so much to ask?" Her soft words in return shook me with the force of an earthquake—words I have heard from her many times since, to other people in different sessions—*"Not even God can change that which is to be your journey on the earth. A child cannot have every whim appeased for its own safety, even though it will be perceived as cruelty. Take heart—God knows better."* Such simple and profound words. Since then, I have heard from different extraordinary souls like St. Dominic and St. Jude, who have told people during sessions not to ask for what we *think* we want, but rather to ask that we have the courage to accept and understand when the right thing is done. These extraordinary souls promise that there is a reason why we must endure the sometimes terrifying struggles we find ourselves up against here, and that at the graduation of our lessons, the method to this madness will be explained to us in perfect detail. In the meantime, the souls will continue with us, to help us find the patience to wait until it is time to know. Some people pray for wellness for themselves or a loved one, not realizing that their illness is the very circumstance that they must cope with and learn from in order to find their magnificent place in the hereafter. Others pray for a temporary happiness when just a little farther down the road, true happiness will be found. The souls want us to know that *everything* we tell them is heard—they will help when it is in our life plan to have what we ask for, and they will stay with us when we grieve over when it is not.

It is so important to the souls that we recognize that no matter what the outcome of things we prayed so hard for, that the right circumstance will happen, and for reasons we may not be able to understand until we find ourselves at the completion of those very lessons. Sometimes, we actually come to understand some of the lessons we endure while we are on the earth, and perhaps even gain some insight into why the struggle is necessary. This is, after all, our goal here—to try and make sense of the senseless and have faith that our life plan is definitive and purposeful. Through so many sessions I have had with families, where the very fiber of their resolve has been tested by difficult circumstances both they *and* their loved ones endured on the earth, the souls have continued to state emphatically that there are no accidental circumstances on the earth—no matter how accidental they may have appeared to us. Just as we are born on a certain day, at a certain time, and through a certain circumstance, so too do we leave the earth. There is a specific reason why we have to suffer, or have to watch helplessly while a loved one suffers. No matter how much we think we could have changed the circumstance of the passing of a loved one, the souls tell us that we do not have that kind of control over the Infinite Light. I have spoken over the years with so many family members who insist that if they had only been more careful, had said no when they said yes, or gotten involved where they didn't, that somehow they could have rewritten the course of the life of their loved ones. The souls haven't the heart to tell us what I know they must be thinking: how foolish and naïve we are to think that somehow we possess a power greater than the Infinite Light to bend the universe to our simple, flawed understanding. We cannot, and we do not have that power, nor would we want it if we really thought things through. If we could understand from the perspective of the souls in the hereafter, then we would know that *nothing* that happens on the earth is meaningless to the story of our journey here, and *everything* has a purpose, even if it can't be immediately seen by us. There are no victims on the earth—only students, who by their circumstance are fulfilling an important part of their life lesson by enduring whatever this lifetime has thrown in their path. The souls have stated time and again that we can never manipulate the circumstances of life, the only thing we have control of is our own will and the time we have to complete our lessons. The only instance when we would actually have control over the actual *time* of our passing would be if we completed our experiences on the earth *sooner* than was anticipated, through our own perfection of our spiritual lessons here. To us, this sounds like a frightening prospect—the better we are, the less time we will be on earth. The souls, in their marvelous world of reward, offer their own perspective: the better we learn here, the less time we will have wasted, and the sooner we graduate to something better. It is only the people who have suffered on the earth, through loss or circumstance, that truly understand what the souls are trying to say. Earth is a complex series of experiences designed to test our faith, our endurance, and our capacity to give and receive love. Some are joyful experiences, but many are tough, and it is up to us to decide whether we will use the time we have to our best advantage or fritter away the experiences, having learned nothing of value from them. No matter when the time comes in our lives, at the time it is necessary for us to graduate out of our existence here, our circumstance of passing is chosen to have the greatest impact on both our own spiritual lessons and the lessons of those around us. No matter what the circumstance, whether through illness or "accident" or at the hands of another—the circumstance of our passing is only the vehicle that transports us from this dimension to the next one.

I have always found it curious that the souls never seem to spend too much time detailing the manner of their passing during a session, and seem to only relay the pertinent facts as a way of proving to their loved ones that they were aware of the circumstance. We tend to regard the moment of death as a monumental tragedy, but the souls regard it as merely the transition to their new life in the hereafter. I didn't realize until I was told by the souls that the circumstance of passing was really not an important step in the story of the soul's transition—it is just the manner in which they were transported to a new life. Ask any married couple about their wedding, and while they can tell you in minute detail about that wonderful day, very few will even remember the ride to the church.

If the souls spend any time at all communicating the details of their passing, it is usually because they want to give us the respect of re-enacting a major moment in *our* life—*their* passing to the hereafter. Otherwise, like their physical bodies, the last moments of their time on earth are no longer of any consequence to the souls—what they have now is all they need. One very resourceful young soul in the hereafter helped both myself and her sister understand the concept though her analogy: She asked us to *"imagine being slapped and pulled physically from a ratty apartment, then shoved hard into a beautiful palace. Once you see that you got a beautiful palace out of the deal, who cares what it took to get you there?"*

People who have had the hard experience of watching a loved one suffer have a very difficult time finding any value in what the souls insist is one of this lifetime's greatest learning experiences. Most cannot find any benefit whatever in having to stand by idly, unable to help, knowing that there is nothing they can do, and feel that suffering is the final insult their loved one will have to face before dying. In fact, many people I have spoken to throughout the years have found the experience of their loved one's suffering (and their own, witnessing it) to be among the cruelest, incomprehensible events of life. But the souls have often said that not only was the "momentary" (in the soul's eyes) suffering a quick, final, worthwhile experience that brought them great spiritual reward in the hereafter, the experience of having watched helplessly as they suffered will prove to be a great spiritual lesson for us on the earth. The souls tell us that the very act of caring and waiting and watching—and not completely abandoning our hope—is one of the most spiritual of the lessons we will ever learn. They also, without fail, will tell their families that great progress in each member's own spiritual journey has been made, because they have *survived*—they have lived through the torment and agony, and yet still continue to live as best they can after falling so hard. I watch the faces of the people in the session, because I know it is neither what they expected to hear, nor is it what they wanted to hear. Nonetheless, the souls want it understood that there is very good reason why we must endure difficult and often painful experiences, both during our lifetime and at the end of it. And they tell us that not only is it incumbent upon us to accept that there was a reason (and a very good one) for all the suffering we and they endured, but experiencing the difficult times and living on here provides perhaps the greatest lesson of our lifetime— to rebuild hope after it has been shattered.

SUCCESS IS IN THE MEASURE OF A SOUL

One of the things that most concerns all of our loved ones in the hereafter about life on earth, is the fact that we are using the wrong yardstick by which to measure our success on the earth. We here tend to think of success in terms of financial abundance, power, or fame. The souls are here to tell us that none of those things matter, or are even important, to consider ourselves successful in our journey on the earth. Sometimes, that kind of success has even become an obstacle because it tends to cloud our purpose here and get in the way of the real quest for success in completing our life lessons here.

I have known very few people who the world considers truly successful that are actually content about their spiritual success on the earth. Nobody who is famous, rich, or important actually has the arrogance, in the quiet of their own heart, to think that they have been afforded an easier path here on the earth. Most times, I have found, it is the complete reverse. With notoriety, money and importance come more problems to face, and more opportunities to fail. I could find no more poignant example of this than the story attributed to John D. Rockefeller, patriarch of the famed Rockefeller family. Near the end of Rockefeller's life—frail and in poor health—he asked to be brought to the construction site of the fabled Rockefeller Center as it was being built in New York City. He had arrived at the site just in time to hear the lunch whistle blow, and the construction men came down off the skeleton of the building to eat their sandwiches in the rubble of steel and concrete, which still surrounded the site. Watching the men laughing with each other as they ate filled Rockefeller with great emotion, and he demanded to be wheeled to the spot where they ate. When the workers saw him coming, the stunned men rose to their feet. But Rockefeller waved at them from his wheelchair to remain seated. He was wheeled to a man sitting among the others, who froze when Rockefeller came in front of him. "Sir," Rockefeller addressed him, "I have spent my lifetime in the pursuit of wealth and power, and I have achieved it. Today, I would give my entire fortune to do as you do now—to eat a sandwich with my own hands."

It seems a sad fact of life here that we are constantly looking over the fence into our neighbor's yard to gauge our own standing. So many of us tend to discount the riches that we actually have, because they seem to have no value in society's eyes. Many people never seem to be satisfied with the life they are given—they think that somehow, someone has it easier than them, and has been blessed with a set of circumstances that *seem* more pleasing. These "blessed" circumstances, however, are only a facade of a life that sees exactly the same pain, struggle, and need for solace as any other circumstance on the earth. Notoriety doesn't make the road here any easier—it is only a different life lesson for some of us here. Handling success, and growing spiritually in *spite* of it, is one of the lessons many will have to endure in their lifetime on the earth.

I have to laugh when people treat me as if *I* am a celebrity. People are so grateful for the communication from their loved ones, that they tend to forget that I am only the instrument—their loved ones are the true stars of the show. It is *their* words that help people here cope and continue, but because of the ability to hear the souls, I get the credit. I consider any success I have in this lifetime useful for only one reason—to find a higher platform that the souls can speak from in order to help more people understand that "death" is not the end of life. To me, the interest I receive from people in television and radio only serves the needs of the souls. If it were really up to me, I would be too happy to go through my life here in anonymity. I have been told by the souls that part of my lesson on the earth is to be in a spotlight, regardless of my sometimes crippling shyness. I was in Burbank, California, recently to tape a television show, where I demonstrated my ability by relaying the souls' messages to their loved ones in the studio audience. After the taping, a young producer ran up to me, gushing, "Oh, Mr. Anderson, you are *so* lucky—I wish I could be you for about ten minutes." I smiled, but in my mind I thought, I *also* wish he could be me for about ten minutes—never being allowed to have an "off" day in my work, having to deal with people who tell me to my face that I am doing the "devil's work," and keeping my feelings from being hurt when people berate me for charging money for my "God-given" ability, as if I could maintain a full-time job *and* work with the bereaved as much as I do now. Yes, I thought—the ten-minute break would be nice sometimes. People only see what they want when they see "success." The producer's words haunted me later that evening—I went to a book signing, staying longer than I was supposed to so I could squeeze in a little more communication from the souls for the people who had attended that evening. We got back to the hotel only to find that the restaurant was long closed, and there wasn't another place open for miles—our dinner that evening was a bottle of soda and a packet of peanut butter crackers from the hotel vending machine. I thought to myself that I wish I could be a guy that had a decent dinner for about ten minutes. I understand that my gift back from the souls for my work with them is the feeling that I have helped someone cope with their loss, and it is a gift I treasure, but nothing is ever as easy as it seems.

In my career as a medium, I have experienced just about every circumstance of life possible through the people who have come to me for a session. I have met people from nearly every walk of life—from the exceedingly wealthy to the terrifyingly poor, from royalty and movie stars to simple, decent working people, and from highly educated to illiterate. I have found one thing, however: no matter what their status in life, *everyone* suffers when they experience loss. No one can buy or negotiate their way out of experiencing the pain and anguish that accompanies any type of loss. The souls, during the course of every session, have helped to illustrate for me that there are places we will stumble on our road through life here, regardless of whether the road is paved in gold or packed with dirt. We all will have to grieve; it is perhaps the one thing all of us on the earth have in common. Nothing makes that road easier, except for our own willingness to get up, brush ourselves off, and try to continue to hang on to our hope while we stumble through tragedies in our lives. Sometimes the more we have in material trappings makes the fall that much harder to deal with. The souls have often told me that one of the hardest things on the earth to deal with is success because it brings with it a much higher level of expectation than most people will have to encounter. Some things are different for the truly successful— the fall to failure is from a much higher place, and the results are more devastating. Also, and much harder to understand—the successful and famous are not afforded the same space to grieve as the rest of us. I often think about the truly famous who have to suffer the loss of a loved one in a very public way. One famous comedienne I know had to go back to work immediately following her loss, making other people laugh in spite of her pain. It can never be as easy as it is made to look. There have been many people who are considered famous that have come to see me for a session. What I find interesting is that when they come, they are no longer "famous"—they are just bereaved people hoping to find comfort. Loss is a very humbling experience, no matter who you are in this lifetime, and no matter how many people can recognize your face or work. When they come to hear from their loved ones, they come only as bereaved people. I am always grateful, however, for the celebrities who make at least part of their sessions with me public, because it helps so many people understand that they are not alone in how they are coping with their losses, and also because it illustrates, like nothing else, that no matter how many people we know, or know us, we are the real star in the movie of our lifetime on the earth, and that no matter what life brings us in the way of popularity, or wealth, or importance, only our need to walk our own road is important.

The souls have told me that the true "stars" of this existence go largely unnoticed by the world, until they find themselves in the glory of the hereafter. Why? Because we operate from a different set of values here than that of the Infinite Light. The souls want us to know that *no* kindness done to another is ever forgotten by the hereafter, and our finest moments on the earth are spent in service to others. The Infinite Light prizes humility in the kind and loving things we do for each other, things that never seem to be noticed by anyone but have a profound effect on our spiritual growth while we are on the earth. Through so many of the session I have done, I have found that our loved ones draw the most attention to our actions in the times of our greatest adversity. Our greatest accomplishments happen at the darkest moments of our lives, when even in spite of the fact that our hearts are heavy, we still have some love and compassion left for others. Those are the moments when our loved ones in the hereafter are the most proud of us—these simple, often unacknowledged kindnesses are the stones in the path that bring us closer to our spiritual perfection.

There are very few times in the course of communicating that the souls will caution about some of the choices we make in our lives. The souls do warn, however, that we must be very careful when we believe that power, money, and fame will make us better people, and then run blindly in search of what we perceive is "success" on the earth. Like the biblical passage that says, "What does a man profit if he gains the whole world, only to lose his soul?" the souls tell us that it is just as easy to subvert our path here, through the relentless pursuit of riches, as it is to veer off the road because of our choice to turn away from our purpose. I have met many people considered powerful, wealthy, and famous by the standard of the earth, but their success in the eyes to the Infinite Light can only be measured by the power of love they possess, their wealth of kindness, and their value to others whose lives they have enriched. These are the only true riches, and each of us has it within us to create spiritual riches beyond belief.

I still think back to my earlier days, when in my own time of struggle, Mother Cabrini told me, *"We cannot promise you reward in this lifetime— only in the next."* We are the true heroes and heroines of this existence, whether the successes of our lives are recognized by others, or not. Our greatest fans are the souls in the hereafter, who cheer our accomplishments and encourage us to be the best we can be while we are here, and they reward the greatness of even the most humble acts of love and kindness in a way they promise will surpass even the wildest success on the earth.

THE SOULS HAVE NEVER LEFT US

I have had many opportunities, through the many extraordinary people who have come for sessions over the years, to understand how enduring love can be, and how truly difficult it is to live day to day without someone we love. Often during a session a family member will ask me, "Do they know how much we love and miss them?" My first instinct is to answer for the souls in my typically candid manner, "Of course they do—why do you think they are communicating?" Instead, and before I can open up my big mouth, the souls will answer in a surprisingly emotional and heartfelt way, *"We are closer to you than we ever could have been on the earth, and we will never abandon you."*

One of the most important messages that the souls have implored me to tell people is that they have *never* left us. I always thought this statement would go without saying, because these souls were our friends, our lovers, our husbands and wives, our brothers and sisters, and our sons and daughters on the earth—they wouldn't abandon us on the earth, so why would they disappear from us just because they have moved to another dimension? But in the passing of a loved one, more than just an emotional loss has taken place—a physical presence that once roamed the earth is no longer here. When we are grieving the loss of a loved one, what proof is there that our feeling of being alone is not actually reality? It is such an easy pit of despair to fall into, and the very reason why the souls, without fail, have mentioned it in every single session I have done for more than twenty-seven years, in one form or another—*"I am always with you."*

Now that the souls have made their transition and understand this world in a way that was impossible to understand while they were on the earth, they can see their loved ones here in a way they never could have imagined. Instead of looking from the outside and guessing about what is in our minds and hearts, they now have the ability to understand us better than we understand ourselves—our hopes, our fears, our struggles, our feelings, and our motivations. They now see us, stripped of the arrogant, brave, prideful, stoic mask we wear on the earth, and see into the actual *souls* we are, and the souls we will become. Their hope is to become a kind of "guidance counselor" to us to quicken the process of our understanding about the experiences we must go through on the earth, and to help us avoid the pitfalls of hopelessness and despair, if it is at all possible. Part of the ongoing spiritual journey of any soul that has passed on is their willingness to reach one hand toward the Infinite Light, yet also reaching back to earth, to create a bridge of hope for us— becoming our link to the path we need to follow.

The souls prove by their very appearance in the sessions I do that they have never left us. My ability is such that I cannot conjure or *call* any of the souls to appear—they do that on their own. Since they have been following us on the earth, they know that their loved ones here have sought out the opportunity where they will be near someone who can pick up, or discern, the communication of the souls. This is also the reason that I do not allow people attending a session to tell me whom they want to hear from and why; the souls want the opportunity to prove that they already know what is important, and the questions their loved ones are hoping to have answered. When they can, the souls will make reference to our lives since their passing, if only to illustrate once again that they are still part of the family, and interested in the day-to-day issues we still deal with. They ask us to think of them not as *gone*, but rather, as in a "foreign country," where although our communication with them is limited, they still have the opportunity to reach out to us when it is necessary. By the same token, the souls tell us that no matter what manner we communicate to them—whether in the silence of our hearts or out loud, they hear *everything* we tell them. They have been listening, and even if they cannot answer us in a way that is physically palpable to us, they can still answer us—often in ways we can't readily comprehend. It is sometimes very disheartening for me to get letters and calls from people who are desperate to have a session so that they can let their deceased loved ones know that they are sorry, or that they forgive them, or that they didn't mean to be hurtful or insensitive to them when they were on the earth. These people eat themselves alive with guilt, thinking that because their loved one is no longer on the earth, somehow they have lost their opportunity to make amends. Or worse, that somehow I am the only conduit by which they can get their apology across. I'm not. The souls say over and over, *"I am closer to you than you can imagine,"* and the souls mean it literally. Now that they are in the hereafter, they understand the sensitivities, struggles, and problems in our minds and hearts. The souls are way ahead of us—they understand, forgive, and help us to understand and forgive ourselves. They are indeed closer to us in the hereafter than they ever could have been on the earth. Talk to your loved ones when you need to—they will always be listening.

I truly believe that receiving messages from the souls is a miracle, not because it is possible, but because of the profound effects these messages can have on our lives. Although the souls insist they cannot and will not control the course of our lifetime here, I have seen so many incredible instances where their very presence in our lives help us define our own reason for being here. By the same token, part of the soul's ongoing spiritual education in continuing with us is to understand their *own* motivations when they were on the earth. The souls have told me that sometimes the most profound understanding of life here cannot happen until we have left the earth and can see why the world dealt us the circumstances it did. It goes a long way in helping the souls to understand choices they made in life and goes an even longer way in helping us to understand, forgive, and move forward with our experiences on the earth.

Although I did not know him at the time, I remember very well the day my good friend Daniel Zehrer was born—that day was also my seventeenth birthday. It is so odd how life will sometimes throw the unlikeliest people together in order to help us learn one life lesson or another. Besides a huge gap in our ages, we could not be more physically different—Dan is a bodybuilder, the size of two men tied together at the waist, and I am, well, not. But what we lack in physical similarity we make up for in attitude—Dan is a good-natured, kind, thoughtful, and caring soul, but our amount of patience with this world combined wouldn't fill a teaspoon. Dan has known for quite some time that he was adopted at the age of nine months, and has never been particularly interested in finding his birth parents, except, perhaps, for mild curiosity about other siblings, nationality, and the like. Although he has made it clear that he need not look any further than the people who adopted him to find his "parents," a recent diagnosis of a congenital heart problem prompted him to perhaps think about researching his birth family's medical history. After finding out the names of his birth parents, who were unmarried at the time of his birth, Dan had a change of heart and decided to leave his medical condition in hands of fate and not intrude on their lives some thirty years later.

It has become an unofficial custom that on Thursday evenings after the sessions, Dan, my assistant, Dianne, myself and whatever friends are available will meet at our favorite Japanese restaurant to discuss the week's events. During the course of the discussion one evening during dinner, I looked at Dan, but I was drawn to an energy and light that I saw appear around him. Standing behind Dan, with his hands on Dan's shoulders, appeared the figure of a man. He just stood there beaming. I watched him curiously. I had done a session for Dan previously, and had never seen this man before, but he brought with him a strong feeling of family. When he saw that he had my attention, he said, *"I am Dad."* I panicked for a moment, thinking, "Good Lord, Dan's father has passed on tonight," but I looked at the figure again, and it was not the man I knew to be Dan's father. I thought in my mind, "You're not Mr. Zehrer, I *know* Dan's father," but he quickly clarified his statement by telling me, *"No, no—I am Dad—his birth father."* He looked down at Dan the way a father beams at his newborn son for the first time—with such joy and pride that it actually filled my heart with such immense joy as well. He was so overwhelmed at seeing what a fine man his son turned out to be that it caused a moment of melancholy in him. He spoke in such an apologetic tone, *"I never had a chance to see him, and I didn't have a say in the decision to give him up. Things were different then. This is my son."* I found myself caught up in his emotions and also found myself overwhelmed by his joy in having found something that was missing for so many years. His father went on to explain to me that he had just recently passed on, and was on the earth as part of his Life Review to see the boy he was deprived of seeing in his lifetime on the earth. Although I have heard from many souls in the course of my years, this was the first time a soul appeared to me who was in the middle of his Life Review—the living movie of our life where we come to understand all the things that eluded us on the earth before making the transition to the other side. Dan's father's emotions connected so strongly to my soul because he hadn't fully made the transition to the spiritual world yet, and his emotions were still of the earth. It was an incredible experience—to feel that pride and immense joy, even the melancholy ache—burn in my heart as if they were my own emotions. This man needed Dan to know that he was loved by his birth mother and father, and it was only through circumstance that they could not be married and raise Dan as their son. The man disappeared as quickly as he appeared, and time seemed to resume again around me. I waited a few minutes to tell Dan what had happened, and he listened very carefully and with great interest to this spontaneous communication. I think it will take some time and reflection for Dan to fully understand the emotional significance of this apparition, and although he is a strong man, there will come a time when he will grieve the loss of the father he did not know, but who loved him so much he needed to touch Dan from the hereafter. Nonetheless, after thirty years of wondering, his birth father had an extraordinary opportunity to say the words he needed to say. The souls tell us constantly that even if it takes a lifetime, the issues that haunt us on the earth will find their peace in the hereafter, and as much as they help us to continue on the earth, we also help them to continue spiritually in the hereafter.

YOU WILL NEVER BE FORGOTTEN

There was a man who came to a group session with his daughter. His wife of twenty years recently passed on from breast cancer, and it was obvious to me during his wife's communication from the hereafter that he was still in a very desperate state of grief. Normally I try to tell as many people who will listen *not* to come to hear their loved one's communication until some perspective has returned, and the physical loss is not still such an open wound. The problem is that I have no idea who will be at these groups or why, so I have to trust the attendees that they are not hoping to have the impossible happen—to dupe their hearts into thinking that since their loved ones are communicating, they have never left the earth. As his wife began communicating that evening, I watched his expression go from amazement, to despair, and then to anger. His fists began to clench as I talked, and his lip began to quiver. The last thing I told him was, "Your wife wants me to assure both you and your daughter that during your pain, she has never left your side."

The gentleman's face reddened and grew taut. "And they let you get away with that?"

"I beg your pardon?" I honestly thought I had not heard him correctly.

"You heard me," he continued brusquely. "You dispense those generic statements like candy; you tell that to everybody."

I, his daughter, and the rest of the people in the group looked at him, wide-eyed and stunned. For a second, I felt like I had fallen into a parallel universe, and right into the contestant's seat on the "Who Wants to Shoot the Messenger?" show. His wife in the hereafter, already one step ahead of my thought process (thank goodness) told me to *look* at him. I didn't see a rude, angry man anymore—I saw a confused, scared, heartbroken husband and father, who didn't know how he was going to survive his loss and be two parents to his young daughter.

"Your wife states again that during your pain, she has never left your side. If she has to say that to infinity *and beyond*, it will never be enough times."

He stared at me quizzically, and his daughter looked at him, surprised. "Thank you," he said, calmly.

Luckily for me, that was the last session in the group that evening. His statement rattled me. I have been working for more than a quarter of a century with the souls in the hereafter, and some of the things every single soul wants their loved ones here to know is that they are happy, at peace, and for us to understand that they are always with us when we need them. How can I decide to edit what each individual soul wants to tell their individual loved ones, simply because another soul also wanted its family to know the same thing? My job is to listen and report, not edit and check for previous usage. Three days later, I received a voice mail at the office from that gentleman who said, in part, "I sincerely apologize for my outburst, and accusing you of saying the same thing to everybody. Every day of her life, my wife used to tell me, '*I love you—to infinity and beyond.*'" Per usual, the souls know exactly what they are doing.

If I have learned anything from the sessions I do for the bereaved, it is that the souls say what they mean, regardless of whether we hold it to our hearts, or cast it off as "fluff." I can imagine how irritating it must be to the souls to say, "*I have helped you through the roughest obstacles of your life,*" only for their loved ones here to nod and think (as I know some of them do), "Yeah, yeah—come through with your nickname."

At this point in my life, I am settling into middle age as gracefully as I am able. It is too late for me to begin finding clever ways to dress the words of the souls when they make the same statements, and still honor the integrity of what they have come so far to tell us. We will just have to reconcile that the same words will mean different things to each person who hears them. Just because your significant other has told someone *I love you* before meeting you, it does not cheapen the value of those wonderful words when they are whispered to you in trust. It is the same for the souls in the hereafter. They can't get any more creative with their language, so we will have to get smarter about understanding that no matter how many times they are asked, no matter how many times they are called, and no matter how many situations we find ourselves in, our loved ones help captain the ship of our spiritual journey here, at our sides, in our hearts—and to use a phrase that is not mine—for infinity and *beyond*.

The souls of our loved ones are now part of a great universe that affords them the opportunity to be all things at all times. They are part of a realm that has no adherence to the rules of the earth—not of time, not of space, and not of distance. When we need them, the souls are with us. They can walk with us and still continue their spiritual journey.

They can speak to us and listen at the same time. Whenever they are needed, and no matter how often, the souls are there for us to help us get through the rough spots in our struggles here, whether we are aware of their assistance or not. No matter where we are on the earth, and no matter how long—the souls promise us we are never without their guidance, their wisdom, and their love.

5.

SEE–NO
EVIL

A few years back, a woman came to see me who lost her son, Paul, in a boating accident. During the session, Paul wasted no time in communicating to his mother that although he was happy and at peace in the hereafter, he was concerned about her feelings of hopelessness, since he was the last of her family on the earth. His words were encouraging and hopeful. He wanted her to know that no matter where she found herself on earth, he would always be near, and he told her that each day brought her closer to the time when she would see him, her parents, and her beloved pets who will be waiting for her in the hereafter when it is her time to pass. She seemed visibly relieved to hear his words, and thanked me after the session. As she proceeded to the door, she suddenly stopped and turned around, looking concerned. "How do I know that was really my son, and not the devil masquerading as him?" I was stunned at the question, thinking at first it was a joke. She was actually concerned that something or *somebody* evil would have the power to dupe her into believing she was hearing from the boy she gave birth to—someone whose presence she would know in the dark. Who would be able to fool her so convincingly, and what would be the benefit in masquerading as a loved one to communicate messages of hope to people here? Why would anyone here *or* hereafter perpetrate this cruel feat, or even *want* to?

We on the earth have a strange preoccupation with evil. Not the evil that we can see all around us in our everyday lives, but an evil we *can't* see—a kind of supernatural force that is so easy to be blamed when we don't want to face our own failings on the earth. Maybe it is because of my spiritual beliefs, or even because of my relationship to the souls in the hereafter, but I find it so disappointing that people actually believe in an all-encompassing force of evil that is so powerful it rivals the power of God, or the Infinite Light. Take heart if you are one of the people who throw your hands up at the end of the day and retreat by saying "the *devil* made me do it"—the souls want you to know that there is *no such thing*.

Most of us, myself included, have been taught that if you are not kind and good and worthy, your sorry self is sent, without any thought or consideration by God, straight to hell. The threat of eternal damnation is propagated by ill-informed—though probably well-meaning—people who want to believe that if someone wrongs us, hurts us, or does despicable things on the earth, then off to a fiery punishment they go, sent by a vengeful, righteous God forever. It may be a soothing thought; those who made us suffer will suffer themselves, but we have forgotten that there is a force more powerful than our own, with a much better command over right and wrong and a decidedly better perspective than we can ever have on the earth. These same people, who rant and rave that the punishment for wrongs on the earth is swift and mighty, have forgotten perhaps the most fundamental belief they hold—justice is the domain of the Infinite Light. I am baffled when I hear people say that the Infinite Light (or God) knows us, loves us, and understands our struggles, yet in the same breath say that the Infinite Light will turn around and punish us if the relationship gets a little bumpy. We have created a chasm in logic by saying on the one hand, the Infinite Light forgives us if we ask, yet says on the other hand that the price of forgiveness is punishment. The souls have been very specific in their messages about this issue because we have twisted what we hope and what we fear too tightly together with regard to judgment of ourselves and others.

The souls have told me, repeatedly and quite emphatically, that there is *no hell or evil in the hereafter*. Hell is a product of our own zest to see judgment on the earth. The Infinite Light, who knows us at the very fiber of our being, understands the errors we create, the evil we do, and the failures that move us off our path in life. However, in spite of how far we have cast ourselves away from what is our purpose on the earth, the Infinite Light will never abandon us. No matter how badly we have fallen off our course here, the opportunity to correct those mistakes and work toward spiritual goodness once we return to the hereafter will always be there for us. The Infinite Light does not force us to own up to our failings—the souls do it because of the irresistible peace and love that abounds in the hereafter, and *all* souls want to be loved. This promise of peace and love in the hereafter will stir us to want to walk closer to the Light, and the choice will be up to us when and how it will happen. Our free will is as abundant in the hereafter as it is on the earth. We are in the driver's seat, to try, to fail, to accomplish, to waste, to surrender, and to try again.

While knowing there is no punishment in the next life sounds very good for those who have done terrible things on the earth, the souls caution us to understand that *no one* escapes having to reconcile the evil we do while we are on the earth. When we have wasted our opportunities to grow spiritually on the earth, or worse, spent our time here making others suffer, we will come back to the hereafter to understand firsthand how our actions hurt others, and how damaging these things were to our spiritual growth. The earth is very much like a school—we need certain subjects to graduate and move on. If we come to the end of our year without completing all the courses, or even failing some, then we may leave the school, but we will have to make up the courses before we can move on. It is very much the same in the hereafter. Now that we understand the impact of our actions on others once we have graduated from the earth, it will take us time to repeat the life lessons we failed on the earth, before we can move on spiritually with the rest of the "class." We do not experience the full spiritual benefit of the beauty and peace of the Infinite Light until we know we have earned it.

I have asked the souls many times if it is in some of our life plans to create suffering for others on the earth, through violence or some other hurtful act. It is a question they cannot fully answer, because it has so many levels to it that we cannot understand until we have finished our time on the earth. What they can tell us, however, is that the Infinite Light is more powerful than we think. Even with our free will to choose between right and wrong, the Infinite Light already knows who will choose which, and places us or others in the circumstances we will play out. This has been hinted at by some of the souls who have appeared in the sessions, who have passed on because of acts of violence committed by someone else. Once they pass, they seem to understand that it was not purely accidental that they were placed in the path of someone who would cause them harm. They seem more concerned in the session that we understand

and forgive their attackers. This is something that does not sit well with their grieving families here, yet it is what the souls know to be the right thing to do, and they ask us to trust them. It seems that whatever is done on the earth, justice is dispensed on its own terms in the hereafter, and it is not for us to judge what we could never understand.

I have had many sessions in the more than twenty-seven years of hearing the souls communicate, and I can tell you that not every soul communicating has lived a perfect life on the earth. It has happened on occasion that the family of someone who has done terrible things on the earth will come to me to find some kind of understanding to the madness that was their loved one's life. The souls will come through in the session, as they say, *"through the grace of the Infinite Light, who has made the opportunity to communicate possible as part of reconciliation."* The souls are given the opportunity to tell their loved ones that they have taken responsibility for the terrible things they have done, and how truly sorry they are. They are working to reconcile these things, slowly, with the help of other souls and the Infinite Light, to progress closer to the grace and beauty of the Light. *Nothing* is unforgivable in the hereafter, and no matter how bad the crime on the earth, the slow process of undoing the damage and moving closer to the Light is available to all the souls who truly want it. I am sorry if this explanation is disappointing to some, but it is an important part of our spiritual education. I know it is important to us to want to know that those who have wronged us get their "comeuppance," but the souls tell us to keep to our own purpose here, and trust the Infinite Light. Our spiritual growth here is certain if we can, if not forgive, then at least understand.

I have often been asked if I have ever encountered an "evil presence," or how I can tell the difference between a "good spirit" and a "bad spirit."

I can tell you that I have never met a "spirit" I didn't like, because evil has never touched the Garden of Souls and there *are no evil souls*. There are so many tales about people being tormented by "evil spirits" that somehow make it their business to terrorize us on the earth. I am not sure why some feel the need to believe that evil is stronger than good. The souls tell me that there simply is no dark, forgotten realm of souls the Infinite Light has chosen to ignore. There are no demons, goblins, and whatever else we want to call them. They are only manifestations of our own fear of the evil that exists only on the earth. It is our own feeble attempt to justify what we cannot control in our own behavior by saying, "the devil made me do it," in order to avoid accountability.

I do not believe one bit in demonic possession. What I find curious is that not very many religions actually believe we can be "possessed" by an evil force, but the idea sounds perfectly reasonable to some people. The souls have told me that for the duration of our time here, there is only "one soul to a customer" and that no evil force has more power than both the Infinite Light and our own vibrant soul. Our bond with the Infinite Light is too strong for that to even be a possibility, and while there may be a lot of reasons, both physically and psychologically for this "phenomenon" to take place, there is no force of evil *anywhere* that has more power than the Infinite Light.

No matter what I tell people—even people I know well—about what I have learned from the souls in the hereafter, they seem to still have the need to buy into the premise of "evil spirits" who woefully roam the earth, taking over our homes, our lives, our cars, and apparently anything else they can get their hands on. I remember about ten years ago, a woman wrote to me who was frantic because she believed her food processor was possessed by an evil spirit. Three weeks later, the local news reported a recall of the same appliance due to electrical malfunctions in the model. I have a good friend, whom I will only call "Laurel" (although she knows who she is) who called me in a panic one day, needing advice. Her elderly father had passed on after a long, wonderful life. Although the passing of a loved one is difficult no matter how long they lived on the earth, the separation was especially painful for Laurel's daughter, who was very fond of her grandfather, and who helped care for him in his last days on earth. The trouble began, Laurel explained, when her daughter started being awakened at night by strange sounds in the room. She also explained to me that her daughter woke up in the middle of the night to see a *presence* hovering over her. She has since been unable to sleep, and pleaded with Laurel to call me and find out what she could do to rid herself of this evil presence. I listened patiently while Laurel spoke, until I decided I couldn't listen to another word. "You *must* be kidding," I told her flatly. "Did you ever stop to think that it could have been your father coming to his granddaughter, just to let her know that he had made the transition? Did you ever think that he may be around her to help her through her grief because he *cares?*"

"*Ohhhh,*" she said, sighing, "I never thought of that."

I could just hear her father saying, *"This is a fine how do you do—I come in comfort and I'm mistaken for evil!"* The souls may stay with us because they know we need them, but they cannot always help our own fears and misconceptions about the spirit world. The souls will come through to us only to help us—it is never their intention to scare us.

Because of the work I do, I have often been called by media or some research facility to investigate what they consider to be a *poltergeist*, or haunting. I rarely go, but if I do, it is only to state the obvious about a soul's momentary connection to the earth. Sometimes the souls, just before their crossing over to the Light, will pause momentarily between the earth and the hereafter. This can be because they are confused and need a slower transition to the hereafter in order to adjust. All they know is the earth, and until they are ready, the souls and the Infinite

Light will wait until they are comfortable making the transition to the hereafter. It is only a momentary pause, though, but in a realm where there is no time as we know it, *momentary* to the souls could mean many years of time on the earth. In the meantime, the souls still think and act as if they were on the earth—with the same emotions and perceptions, until the feelings of being earthbound begin to fade, and the desire for the peace and tranquility of the Light makes them begin to walk in that direction. Some souls have told me that they are in the hereafter as much as possible, because it is peaceful, happy, and beautiful, yet others will tell me that they stay near the earth to help their loved ones through challenges here. The closer they come to the earth, the more they can be felt, seen, and even heard. And the closer to the earth the souls come, the more they take on characteristics that they had on the earth, including the manner of their speech, their sense of humor, and even their impatience. Why these souls are considered "evil" is beyond me; they simply need a few minutes to collect themselves before moving on to their new life in the hereafter.

Although I swore I would never chase the "ghosts" I already know are just temporarily hovering near or on the earth, I did get a call from my friend, a psychologist, who had a patient complaining about souls that hovered in and near her home. One of the psychologist's concerns was that her patient, Rosalba, was frightened of the images she saw, was not getting any sleep, and was going through a rough time in her life. Part of it, I suspect, although she never said it, was that my friend may have thought Rosalba was making the whole thing up in her stress over her problems. But Rosalba was a bright, articulate executive who seemed to have a genuine issue with something that was going on in her home. She thought, perhaps, if we knew what they wanted, we would be able to resolve whatever was keeping them to the house. Because this psychologist was a trusted friend, I decided to go and find out what the souls had on their minds.

Once inside the house, I knew immediately that this was no hoax, and Rosalba was not crazy. I could immediately sense the souls gathered there. There were many souls around, like a reunion of people who had occupied the house over many generations. Rosalba took me from room to room, explaining the phenomena that she saw and heard. One of the images that disturbed her the most would appear on the living room wall—the face of a man in intense pain, with a type of rope or belt around his neck. Rosalba told me that the image would appear frequently, especially when the house was dark. She also told me that when she was in the bedroom, she felt that she was being watched, and in the basement, she experienced a sense of uneasiness and profound sadness.

We wound up the tour in the basement, where there was the unmistakable "odor of sanctity"—a fragrance the souls sometimes leave behind them as they move through dimensions. Rosalba pointed out a stain in the carpet. No matter what she did, she couldn't remove the stain. She even had the carpet taken up, the floor underneath it cleaned, and a new carpet laid in its place, but the stain reappeared in the same place.

It would be so easy for a story like this to career out of control, and create hysteria. After all, this situation had the makings of a sensational horror film or book. The ingredients are simple: a little bit of phenomena, a touch of history, and a generous helping of media exploitation. I believe that this is what happened in the case of the home of the Lutz family in Amityville, Long Island, that became the basis for the movie *The Amityville Horror.* My belief is that the Lutz home, like Rosalba's house, was simply occupied by souls whose messages were misunderstood and blown *way* out of proportion and thought of as evil.

From listening to the voices around me as I walked through Rosalba's home, it was fairly easy to discern that we were dealing with generations of three different families who occupied the house over time. Not only that, but the souls told me that the house had been built on hallowed ground—the land once belonging to a church that existed not too far from the property. The more the souls spoke, the more sense the whole situation made. There were three distinct circumstances of passing in the house—one accidental, two intentional. It seemed someone fell down the cellar stairs to their death, near the very spot where the recurrent stain could be found. The other two deaths occurred due to suicide and murder. The murder was apparently the result of a marital dispute, again in the basement, and the suicide was a product of a severely depressed soul who had trouble in life trying to make ends meet for his family.

I listened to the souls for as long as I could, and then related the information to Rosalba and the psychologist, expecting them to be stunned by the news. They weren't; in fact, they were way ahead of me. Rosalba had already accessed the town records that showed a church having been erected and torn down nearly one hundred fifty years earlier, and clerk's records showed the transfer of ownership shortly after the death of the home's original owner. The subsequent deaths were also on record.

Although I was glad that the information I discerned from the souls could be verified, the more important part of this experience was that it gave me the opportunity to dispel some of the ridiculous notions many have about "hauntings." One thing I pointed out to Rosalba was that although the souls regularly "visited" the house, they were certainly not *trapped* there, nor were they trapped on the earth. Sometimes, a soul will linger temporarily on the earth if some issues of their lifetime have not been completely resolved, or they might visit regularly if there is a particular affinity for a loved one or location. These souls are perfectly able to move toward the light and back, and temporary lingering for the souls could mean a few hundred years of time on earth, since there is no concept of time in the hereafter. And certainly the souls do not need our feeble attempts to "set them free." If the souls hang around the earth momentarily, out of care for a loved one or simple curiosity about the new inhabitant of a house they once spent their time on earth in, it is certainly not impeding their progression to the light.

I also told Rosalba that the phenomena she was witnessing in her house was not entirely the work of the souls. We are beings of energy, and energy has a power all its own. We tend to throw off energy in normal everyday situations, and especially in times of high emotion, good and bad. Houses collect that energy, and it goes around and around like a carousel until it dissipates or escapes. I have a friend who swears that from time to time, she can still hear an echo of the harp that played the "Wedding March" in her living room where her daughter was married ten years ago. That was a happy bundle of energy that circles the room and replays itself like a tape recorder from time to time. The same thing can be said of the tortured face that appears frequently on the wall in Rosalba's home—it is an unhappy circumstance whose energy occasionally replays itself. The energy takes the form of a sound or an image, but no matter the manner in which it replays itself, it is not at all generated by the souls in the hereafter, or even those who are hanging around for some odd reason. It is one of those pieces of phenomena better credited to physics than to the souls.

Another notion that the souls feel it is important to dispel is that they *never* intend to harm us. When phenomena happens around us, our earthbound mind is unable to comprehend the occurrence, and anything we cannot readily understand, we fear. It is not the intention of the souls to frighten us out of our skins. If an occurrence is material enough for us to witness, either in sound, smell, or movement, it is simply the souls' way of capturing our attention, for reasons we might not understand readily. People who have come to my home have reported seeing an old man with a beat-up hat come down the stairs, or my deceased cat Boo Boo (no pun was intended—honest), and some lucky ones have even reported seeing St. Philomena or hearing her "knock of assurance." Although it may startle them at the time, no one I know has ever thought of it as evil or menacing.

What I found funny about the souls who were hanging around Rosalba's house that evening was that they felt *they* needed protection from *Rosalba.* That's right; *they* were *frightened* of her, and for good reason. These souls lived in a very different time from the twentieth century. Imagine seeing a woman, unmarried, with a painted face, wearing trousers and allowing a gentleman caller in the house without the benefit of a chaperone—well, you could figure the type of character they thought moved into their homestead. Additionally, it made the souls nervous that there was a cat in the house (during many periods in history cats were considered evil) as well as photos and paintings of cats everywhere. The thing that made the souls the most uncomfortable was something I did not notice until the souls pointed it out. Rosalba had a custom-made bed and bureau set, painted in a faux marble finish, which was very stylish and modern. The bureau had apparently been built with a type of square canopy that she removed and placed in the corner. Rosalba had decided to move the bed to the corner of the room and use the canopy as a headboard, with candles and photos on top. The result—although I didn't notice at first—was that the bed, with its marble finish and candles, bore a remarkable resemblance to an altar or a crypt. The souls thought Rosalba was up to no good—judging her not by the standards of their perspective as souls in the hereafter, but rather from the perspective of people *formerly* of the earth. The souls still retained enough of their humanness, being so close to the earth, to actually be frightened by what they saw.

Months later, I heard from my friend the psychologist that although the phenomena had subsided somewhat, Rosalba decided to put the house up for sale. She did not want to have to live by the rules of people who temporarily shared her house, and maybe the souls will have better luck with a different owner until they are ready to move out and into the hereafter.

The souls have already established that there is no evil in the hereafter. So where *is* evil? Look around you. Talk to anyone who has been through the murder of a child, a fleecing by a con artist, or a deception by a loved one—they will tell you with certainty that hell is where they are standing. Evil is a product only of the earth, and no evil can break into the world of the Garden of Souls. It is purely a by-product of smashed hopes and utter failures by some in their journey here. The souls remind us that we all have the free will to choose our path to the Light, but our free will also allows us to veer off the path and, in essence, turn our backs to the things we need to accomplish in order to complete our education here. Everyone on earth knows how much easier it is to lie than to tell the truth, to do nothing when something must be done, and to take rather than to ask. The climb to the high road will always be more difficult than the easy slide of the low road, but it is the very thing that will prove how we accomplished our goals when it is time to leave the earth. It will always be up to us to choose.

6.

LIVING ON—
THE SEASONS
of LOSS

So much of life on the earth is experiential. You can watch, listen, and *try* to understand, but until you have actually *experienced* one of the many valuable lessons that make up our spiritual education here, you can never fully understand the spectrum of uncertainty that comes of finding yourself in a circumstance with no seeable boundaries or rules. Along the way, we will be given tools for navigating the path to understanding our existence here, but the tools of our education on the earth are not perfect—we cannot walk in another's shoes, or see through their eyes, or feel with their hands. It is only through *experience* that we learn, and it is only through the experience of loss that we can accomplish one of the greatest challenges to our learning souls—surviving the loss of a loved one.

In my twenty-seven years of working with the bereaved, I know one thing for certain: loss is the earth's great leveler. No matter what our education, financial status, or social placement, the grief we will experience due to the physical loss of someone we love has the potential to smash our belief system, dismantle our values, and sometimes even crush our hope. In the course of my work, I have truly seen the mighty fall in facing their own loss—doctors who lose their perspective and fall apart, members of the clergy who suffer a crisis of faith, and grief therapists who become emotionally unraveled—all because they spent many years learning how to understand the effects of loss, but had never really prepared themselves for their own personal loss. There is a fundamental difference between *knowledge* and *experience* with regard to loss: we will be moved by the circumstance of another's loss, but we will be devastated by our own.

Although I have worked with the bereaved for many years, I still cannot consider myself an expert when it comes to knowing how, why, and for how long people will grieve after a loss. My *knowledge* comes through hearing the tragic stories of loss from the people I have met in sessions, and through some of my own personal experiences of loss. My most valuable *experience*, however, comes through my ability to hear communication from the hereafter, and hear firsthand from the only real experts in loss—the souls who have already made the transition we know of as death. Only they can tell us the complete story of loss—from the point of view of having *lived* through the entire experience. Hearing the wisdom of our loved ones passed on has an incredible benefit in understanding the process when we look at the panorama of loss, and through them we are given a rare look not only at the end of the road, but at the beginning of the next. And it is only through them that *I* can speak with any authority about how, why, and for how long we will grieve the loss of those we love.

Death, the souls promise us, is only a chapter in their lifetime, but with a very happy ending. It is only a bridge between two great volumes of the epic that is their existence. Death, for those of us who are left behind, becomes the saga of our struggle to understand loss. The souls feel compelled to share their experience of passing in order to make the burden of our loss lighter for us, and to help us understand that death is not *termination*, but rather, *continuation*. Only another who has experienced the entire spectrum of loss can cast any light on the dark, treacherous road of grief that we will all travel at some point in our lives here. The souls know this, and they promise they will be whispering from the sidelines in our loss when we find ourselves losing sight of our path. It is what I tell people in grief, because it is what I have been told. But no matter what I have been *told*, however, about the souls and their desire to help us walk through our grief, I have not yet completed my own journey here, and therefore am not experienced enough to tell anyone where their grief will take them in their desperate voyage, or why. That part of our challenge will only be explained to us when our life lessons are complete. No matter what road we travel to find understanding and peace, though, the souls promise we will *never* be left alone on that lonely road. They have endured a lifetime of struggle on the earth, and have now seen the completed circle of life here. This new knowledge makes them understand just how valuable and *needed* this painful experience will be to our reward when we have finally earned it. To use a silly but fitting expression, the souls have literally been there, done that, and bought the commemorative T-shirt.

When I started communicating messages from the souls so many years ago, I learned very quickly that the souls' ability to help us is incumbent upon *our* ability to listen and learn. Information has no value unless it can enrich us and make our lives here better—and it must come at a time we can understand it fully. The problem is that unless we have an immediate need for their wisdom, we may hear their words but we will not understand them. Sadly, when the words become so desperately needed, they have long since been forgotten. The souls know it is of vital importance to our journey on the earth that we listen to *their* experience, and learn from our *own*, in order to continue on here after suffering a loss. We have a job to do, and we cannot fall down in our grief, halting the education our souls are here for. Most of what is communicated now, when I hear from the souls, is designed to help us learn how to *live* on the earth, and not just survive it. They know we have been sleepwalking through experiences we thought we would never need, only to wake up startled and grasping for answers when a loved one makes the transition to a new life. In loss, we find ourselves completely unprepared to deal with what will be one of the most profound lessons we will ever experience. I have noticed that in the past few years the souls tend to want to spend more time in the sessions, not rehashing the circumstance of their passing, but rather, preparing us for the world we must continue in. This is why the souls have been focusing more on *living* with loss, rather than just *surviving* loss. They know that although their loved one's session with me will last only an hour or so, their loved one's life here will continue for much longer than that. Many people will search for *comfort* in the words of the souls when they find themselves facing the hard reality that nothing on this plane is forever, but it is exactly then that the souls hope we will look to them for *answers* in our quest to understand the only world that is forever—the Garden of Souls. The souls have been employing the reference of a garden to help us see the beginning, middle, and end of a journey we will all have to make in our lifetime here. To help us endure our grief, they use the seasons of the earth as their method to explain loss.

THE SEASONS

Just as there will be many seasons in our lifetime, there will also be many seasons in our struggle to come to terms with loss. Following a year of seasons can help us find where we are in relation to our circumstance. By marking the seasons in our grief, we can better understand how far we have come, and how far we still need to go. The seasons change as our understanding of loss takes root and our ability to cope begins to grow, and they will shape how we continue in the rest of our challenges here. Some seasons will be rich in the satisfaction of accomplishment, and others will be barren and unyielding, but all are valuable and *necessary* in order to maintain a garden that will represent this important milestone in our life's work on the earth.

Autumn

Autumn is a sudden frost—the first moments of our loved one's passing. Life has changed forever, and everything feels strange and unfamiliar. Emotions shift like wind; one moment we feel the warmth of fond remembrance, the next we are startled back into horrible reality. Someone whom we love is *gone*. Forget what you read in dime-store novels and see in the movies—*no one* bears the loss of a precious loved one gracefully, and there is no romance in loss. I have seen too many bereaved people in my work and heard too many stories of loss to think there is any *good* way to experience loss. The physical loss of a human being we hold dear is cruel and ugly. It has the potential to destroy everything we have built on the earth, and it will hurt, no matter how brave you are. I would be a fool to tell you, because of my ability as a medium, that just because I know for sure the souls are well, vibrant, and happy in the hereafter, it can for one second take away the horror of the moment we all will face when someone we love is no longer around to share our existence here, both physically and emotionally. That is the effect human beings have on each other; we miss who we cannot see, or touch or hear, whether it is because our loved ones are in another country or in another dimension. They are *missed* because they are *loved*.

We drift through most of the first days of loss in a fog. We become exhausted to the point of numbness, and time stands at a strange angle to the rest of the world. Even the souls acknowledge this numbness we have been placed under immediately following loss. Many of us are far too fragile of spirit to endure the pain of loss immediately, and the souls have spoken about the merciful Infinite Light, which assists in bending the shape of perception for us—in small doses, in order to create the time and circumstance for us to accept, in increments, what will be impossible right away to accept. We tend to walk around covered by an emotional fuzzy blanket; not quite sure where we are, and not quite sure what is ahead. It takes time to drift through the shock of loss, but eventually the haze begins to clear. After that, in the ensuing hours and days, everything we do is a marathon, done to distract ourselves from what we will soon need to do—to begin to feel loss, and to *grieve*. We will try to put off feeling the pain for as long as our exhausted bodies will let us. It is like the ballad of *The Erl King*—as long as the horse gallops, the child the father is holding will not die. I no longer find it surprising when people tell me they were too busy to grieve the first few days of their loss—there was simply too much to do, and falling apart was a luxury they could not afford. My good friend Elaine Stillwell spent the first harrowing days of the loss of her daughter, Peggy, shuttling back and forth from Peggy's wake to the intensive care unit of the local hospital, were her son, Denis, lay clinging to life. Their car had smashed into an open drawbridge one evening in August, 1986, killing

Peggy instantly. "There was no time to think, and thank God for that," Elaine told me once. Denis died from his injuries four days later.

Eventually, time, space, and the reality of loss will return. There is no barometer to measure how we will handle that moment when our world stops spinning on its axis—the time when our path here veers suddenly and violently into the dark forest of loss, and we recognize for the first time that we are bereaved. Unfortunately, it is also our shock that keeps us from fully realizing that we are living through one of the most profound moments of our lifetime. At the very first precious seconds of our loved one's passing into a field of light, the souls have the ability to reach back to the earth and touch us in a closeness never before possible, creating an incredible bridge that transcends time and space. It is their gift to us—the energy to make it through those terrible moments we will soon face without actually dying ourselves from the pain. Death, like birth, is about a passage to a new life and an incredible journey, and both are born of great pain. The souls reach through the door to help us in our need, but also to touch something within us to give us the strength to continue, and a reason to believe this *cannot* be the end. They know the toughest season is soon to come.

Winter

One of the most tragic points in our life will come when the gripping reality of what it means to be *bereaved* crashes down around us. It may happen sooner, or later, but it will happen. Life changes so much that it is almost unrecognizable to us, like the scene from *It's a Wonderful Life* where Harry runs through the town that looks so familiar, yet has been so horribly changed. It even concerns the souls in the hereafter, because the terrifying reality of loss can push us into a despair that some may never find their way out of. This is the winter of our bereavement—the time when we fall down and can't find a reason to continue. Depression and illness run rampant at this time because we feel helpless and victimized. We have been stolen from, and we curse ourselves for not keeping a more vigilant watch over our precious loved ones. Worse than that, however, is that in this bitter time, we tend to push away friends and loved ones who remain, simply because it is just too painful to feel. We can't handle the responsibility of loving *anybody* again, because the prospect of losing them also and reopening that wound is too frightening to think about. So we become an island unto ourselves in grief, with no outlet for love and care, and no ability to receive it from others.

Another by-product of this realization comes when grief begins to cast a harsh, ugly light onto everything around us. Suddenly everything we know is wrong, everything is a lie, and no one can be trusted. I have seen people in this condition come for a session on many occasions, and I wonder why the souls still communicate their messages, knowing they are not being heard—people don't want to *hear* from their loved ones, they simply want their loved ones—and their own lives—back. In my work I have truly seen the *dead*, but they are not in the hereafter—they are here, on the earth. They are people who are bereft of joy—emotionally spent and unwilling to find any reason to continue to live. They walk through days, weeks, and months of bereavement like zombies—the heart still beats but the soul is immobile. Something, or someone, has to step in to help pull them out of the emotional deep freeze they have placed themselves in, and usually the souls can be counted on to set about a circumstance where it can happen.

I remember so clearly two women who came to see me for a session when I was in Tampa, Florida. They both looked to be no older than their mid-twenties, but there was a distinct difference in their personalities. One of the woman smiled as she entered and shook my hand; the other stared straight past me and sat on the sofa. Within a few seconds of their sitting down, the soul of a young male appeared in the room, making a gesture as if apologizing to one of the women.

"This young man asks me to tell you that he is sorry for leaving you, but it was his time." I tried to catch the woman's attention, but she just stared out the window. Her friend looked to her for some kind of reaction, but there was none. Feeling that the woman was perhaps dragged here under duress by her friend, who seemed most interested in the session, I focused my attention on the friend and waited for the young man to continue. Again he appeared, but told me his message was for the woman who refused to listen. "Miss," I said, trying to get her attention. "Did you hear me? The young male says the message is for *you*."

The woman turned to me, stone-faced. "Okay."

"This young man tells me you are madder than hell at his passing."
"Okay."

The soul seemed insistent that I press on in spite of the woman's apparent lack of interest. "He tells me that he wishes with all his heart that you weren't mad at him, and he says you will understand one day."

There was no acknowledgment this time, but the soul continued. "He says he is your sweetheart. Tells me he you two are married in the heart and that will never change."

The woman's face tightened into a mask of tension, and she opened her mouth to answer, but no sound came out. She turned away and looked out the window as her friend cried next to her.

I got concerned. "Is everything okay?" I asked her. I had seen many reactions in sessions, but she looked as if she were going to break into a million pieces. Her body and face were so taut.

"Go ahead," she managed to say.

The session went on to reveal a heartbreaking story of this young man who was killed by a drunk driver in the early morning hours of their wedding day. The young man showed me the image of Miss Havisham in *Great Expectations* sitting alone in her wedding dress, waiting for her love to return. He told me that he felt like he ruined her life, and that her grief has made her bitter and uncaring. "He says you've stopped living, and he blames himself for that. He asks you to forgive him for moving ahead of you to the hereafter, but he says he still wants to marry you, and he will be there waiting at the church when it is your time to come."

It is so tragic to see a woman that young with the weight of such tragedy on her shoulders, but I could sense from the young man in the hereafter that there is no way to reach her until she is ready to cope with her loss, her anger, and her hurt. He told her in the session not to let this be her undoing, and that she has to grieve for what she has lost and try to heal. She remained stone-faced, but I could see that her eyes were moist.

We finished the session, and the woman rose and shook my hand. She apologized for her behavior, but she told me that she was just not ready to hear. She could not let go of the gripping anger and feeling that she has been left with nothing. The only thing I could tell her is that her fiancé cared so much about her mental, physical, and spiritual health, and at the very least, to learn from this experience so that she can progress that much quicker here and see her sweetheart again when it is her time. Sometimes there is nothing that can be said; grief has no calendar and no fixed way of knowing how and when the circumstance will be right to begin acceptance and understanding of our loss in order to continue living and learning.

It is not often that I see the wheel of loss turn full circle in the lives of the people who come to me for a session; most people leave and go on with their lives. Sometimes I meet people whose very lives are linked with mine so that I can follow the story of coping with loss in order to get a clearer picture to tell others faced with the same problems.

My friends Mary and Jim first came to see me in 1994 after the loss of their eight-year-old son, Colin, from leukemia. We have remained friendly ever since. The one thing that impressed me from not only the first session, but the subsequent ones as well, is that this bright, articulate, and fun-loving boy would always express his concern about his parents needing to get over the anger and pain in order to move forward. One thing that seems to appear in all of the sessions I have done for them is their son's admonishment, *"Stop beating yourselves up. What makes you think that going over it again and again will make anything change?"* Advice from the hereafter is not always immediately understood until there comes a time when our circumstances make it crystal clear.

I would usually see Mary and Jim every year when I came to do sessions in Michigan. Every time we got together, we would get caught up on the latest things that were going on in each other's lives, their daughter's bloom into young adulthood, and naturally, Colin. Life seemed to be returning to normal for them after his passing. We always had a wonderful time together, but I started to notice differences in both their personalities each time we got together. They were still the wonderful, fun-loving, and kind people I always knew, but in the odd moments of our conversation when things got a little more personal, Jim seemed a little more distant, and Mary seemed a little less sure of herself. I know that coping with loss is a series of one step forward and two steps back sometimes, but this was different. Something seemed to be brewing, but I felt I had no right to involve myself personally in their affairs.

When they planned a trip to New York in the fall of the following year, I was so excited to know they were coming. When I met them at the airport, however, it was clear to me that there was something wrong. Mary seemed tense and unsure, and Jim was distracted and overly enthusiastic. Something seemed off, but there were moments during the weekend where I saw glimmers of the Mary and Jim that I always knew. Those moments didn't last long, though. The tension between them was incredible, and they interacted with each other as if they were strangers who witnessed the same horrible crime. Although we all tried to pretend everything was all right, I knew that they were falling apart. They talked more about Colin and days gone by, and about how much less sure they were about the world around them. They were losing their grip on their ability to cope, and the pain was driving a wedge in their relationship. The loss that bound them together as a family was now pulling them apart.

People grieve differently when faced with the same loss. We never know how we will react until the time comes. Some of us will be sinkers, and some will be swimmers. Some will cry often, others will be stunned into silence. Some will go outside of themselves for consolation, and some will pull tightly inward, away from the world. The time I spent with Mary and Jim showed me that they were no longer able to pull each other through their grief, and neither one liked what the other had become. It seemed to me that Jim was no longer able to carry the burden of Mary's grief as he had in the beginning, because his own grief was too much for him. Mary did not know how to reach into her husband, who had pulled his own grief inward in an effort to keep it from destroying him. The more she wanted to confront it, the less he wanted to deal with it. They were growing apart in their ability to cope—Mary wanted to keep their loss at the forefront of their relationship in an effort not to forget, and Jim wanted to bury the memories and his pain in an effort not to re-member. It was the coldest of all times in the seasons of their grief— Mary and Jim were *tired.* They were tired of crying, tired of fighting, and tired of being bereaved.

Coming to terms with the prospect that the bereavement is a life-long commitment is a slow and sometimes difficult journey in itself. I am as concerned about those who tell me they quickly recovered from their grief as I am of those who tell me they cannot seem to recover from their grief. The process of learning to live as a bereaved person, and accepting the great challenge of this life lesson, is something that will take patience, understanding, and help from our loved ones in the hereafter. Time is equal to perspective when we think about learning to cope. Just like a scar, grief will lessen in severity over time—some days will be better than others, but each day will make a difference in building the resolve we need to continue on our path. But no matter how well it feels, the scar will never completely disappear—we are bereaved for the rest of our lives. Mary and Jim had a revelation—loss had taken their son, but they would not allow loss to take everything else they hold dear. After a short separation, they are together again and are learning how to live *in addition* to their loss, both individually and as a couple. I think they are beginning to understand that loss takes a second to happen, but a lifetime to comprehend. With patience and understanding, they have decided to mend—each at his own pace, but together.

It takes the most incredible strength of courage to not just lie down and die spiritually, leaving the rest of our lives here as wasted time on the earth. The souls can help us to continue walking, but they cannot make us face the challenge of this dark time. It must be our choice to continue risking emotional pain by living again. So the souls wait, watch, and hope. They wait for us to cry until we cannot cry another tear, to scream until there is no more sound, and to swing our arms blindly until we are exhausted by the futility. The souls will wait until we reach the critical moment when we must decide to face fear again, to face feeling again, to face life again.

Spring

I often think that the tragedy of loss is like a terrible storm, where everything we knew and understood is battered by furious waves of despair that threaten to consume us at any moment. Somehow, though, in this great storm, something happens within us—some fundamental instinct to *survive* rises up within us to help carry us until we can regain our footing. Something seems to awaken in our own souls that tells us the storm *will* gradually lessen, and the sun might actually begin to peek from behind the still-threatening clouds. There is something about us as beings that makes us, perhaps even unconsciously, *want* to lean toward the sun; to acceptance, understanding, and peace. It is the spring in our seasons of loss, and it is time to allow ourselves to find the sun.

Sometimes the milestones in our journey to acceptance of loss are imperceptible until we look back and see just how far we have come from where we started. We literally allow life to begin again for us; not quite the life we knew, but a life we are still able to live. The process of learning to cope is a series of small steps; first feeble and tenuous, then more assured, as we begin to rediscover the value of continuing again in our path on the earth.

The emotions we begin to experience in the spring of our acceptance are the first signs of the re-awakening from the winter of our grief. Although they are uneven and raw, they are necessary in helping us to feel again. The ability to cry and reveal the effects of a broken heart goes a long way in helping us to survive loss; the souls have often said that crying washes the soul clean. As we begin to hobble toward understanding, we will travel through a myriad of tunnels before returning to the road that is our life plan.

Dr. Risa Levenson Gold, a psychiatrist and dear friend of mine, has been an inspiration to me and many others for her insight into the process of coping with loss and learning to find peace again. She explains the cycle of emotions with her characteristic clarity:

In the field of psychiatry, everything that one feels in his or her life is a key which opens up another door within them. It is very much the same after loss. It is not surprising that we experience such anger after suffering the loss of a loved one.

Our initial need is to blame—whether it be ourselves or someone else. We have to justify tragedy, so we look to someone or something to pin our emotions to in an effort to bring a sense of balance to an event that we have no understanding of. The anger that comes out of blame is like an acid that will bore through every value we have unless we can neutralize it with understanding.

I had a patient whose husband was killed in an apparent car-jacking. Although she is on the slow road of coping with her loss, her heart blames everyone who she feels is responsible for her loss. Her biggest obstacle in dealing with the loss of her husband will be the Herculean task of erasing the dark anger she feels, and her need to blame and make someone accountable for her pain.

Anger is not time well spent when you are suffering after loss. Some people have told me that their anger helps focus them through the coping process and gives them a reason to continue, if only to seek justice. The best way to deal with anger after loss is to channel it into something productive. When the anger has subsided (if it ever does), the process of dealing with the pain can begin. If you feel anger about a tragic occurrence in your life, ask yourself what is to be gained by the feelings of hate and dread. Rather than dwell on something that can never be erased, set about the process of learning to feel peace again. So much can be gained by focusing on that which will eventually change rather than that which never can change. Your emotional well-being will be the better for it in the long run.

Many people who come to some of the group sessions I do suddenly discover that they are not alone in their grief, in their blame, in their anger, or in their desire to find peace. Some people find that their circumstance of loss is not unusual, and that there are people who want to share the special bond of loss with other bereaved ones. Part of recovery after loss is coming to the realization that you are not alone in your struggle to cope. Feelings of isolation are so strong after loss that the souls in the hereafter have encouraged me to find more ways to bring the bereaved together; there is truly strength in numbers, and with strength comes hope. One of the greatest achievements of the twentieth century is that we have abandoned the notion that no "laundry" should be aired in public. We have just begun to talk openly about our problems, and seek people who we know will understand. We have resources and programs for just about every kind of human concern—nothing is relegated to the dark closets of shame anymore when people are hurting. Resources are everywhere to help people who are struggling with loss, but they only work if we are willing to take a chance on ourselves and trust others with our pain. Just like the souls remind us, we are not alone in our struggles with them by our side; we need never feel we are alone in our grief on the earth.

Among the most profound messages I receive from the hereafter are those that come in an effort to help us understand that not everything on the earth has a cure. There is no cure for loss, and no perfect mending of a broken heart. It is like a physical condition we discover that we must resign ourselves to live with, or live in spite of. The souls can offer no more quick fixes for the feelings of grief we have than anyone else. The only thing they can help us understand is that we will not have to cope with our struggles alone.

Many people in the sessions have a hard time accepting when their loved one in the hereafter tells them, *"Go on with your life."* It is not the answer they wanted. Somehow they wanted the directions, the keys to the car, and someone to drive them. They come to the sessions hoping the souls will give them a secret recipe for understanding the meaning of every struggle they will face. The souls always find our disappointment amusing—like the mail boy asking the owner of a corporation where he can sign up for the job of company president. They have gone through a lifetime of struggle, and now it is *our* turn to use their experience of completion as a tool, as a map, and as an inspiration for our own accomplishment here. They can help in many ways, but they cannot walk the road for us—that is entirely up to us. In one session, the father of a young man who came for answers encouraged his son to find a way to continue on his road here without his father's physical presence. "How?" the young man asked, intending to push the envelope. Actually, I was also interested in hearing what this soul would tell him, if anything. *"How, indeed,"* I heard his father say. *"How you do it is how it will be done."*

Finding our way back to the path of our life will take us through anger, depression, fear, hatred, and bitterness many times throughout our struggle to cope after a loss. The courage to face the pain is perhaps one of the greatest gifts our loved ones give us from the hereafter, but no matter how much they can coax us to this understanding, they know that the decision to survive loss and continue is ours to make alone. The reward, they promise, will be worth every second of the pain.

Summer

Summer is a warm wind of peace. It is the time in our loss that we can actually look forward to what we have gained, rather than look back to what we have lost. Just as the seasons of the earth go full circle, so will the seasons of our loss. Life will not be normal again; *normal* is a word that passes on with our loved ones. But our lives will eventually become ours. To heal after loss is not to forget the loss of a loved one, but rather, to remember the life of a loved one in a world of grace and beauty.

One of our greatest struggles after loss is to learn how to return to the world of the living after spending so much time in the world of loss. One of the scariest things is to try again—to allow another human being to touch us in love, to be able to laugh without feeling guilt, and to relegate loss from its position of being our reason to live to a reason for having lived. When some perspective has returned, and we are able to see again the full spectrum of our lifetime here, we will understand that our grief is now a part of who we are. Like the memory of our loved ones, grief will never disappear, we just grow stronger to support the weight of it.

Some of the most poignant moments in my work come as a result of meeting people who are trying to begin again after loss. They are desperate to look forward, but never want to lose sight of the past. This is most common when a widower has come to see me after the passing of his wife.

There was a man who came to see me once who needed a friend more than he needed a session. The minute he sat down for the session, he burst into tears, telling me that he was so ashamed at himself for even looking at another woman when his beautiful wife had been so good to him for more than twenty years. But he was lonely, he told me, and he still had a heart full of love. He came seeking not advice, but *permission* from his wife to live again. *"Go on with your life,"* she told him. *"Our love will never die, and I love whoever you choose to give your heart to. You need to live and love again, and besides—you will not survive long eating the meals you cook yourself!"* The words may be wise, prophetic, and sometimes even funny, but the message is the same—it is time to continue. Given the chance, given the hope, and given the courage, life will indeed begin again.

After seeing a distraught family struggling to find peace after their loss, I asked the souls why the loss of a loved one is so difficult, even if we believe with all our heart that the souls are free of every pain we now feel. Their answer was simple and startling, *"Grief is the cost of love."* To say so glibly to someone that they should rejoice because their loved ones are in a better place is an insult to their humanness and their emotions. We grieve because we took a chance in this lifetime, knowing that our loved ones were a gift we couldn't keep forever. Yet we will continue to take the chance because we know in our hearts it will return to us, at a different time and in a different world. The souls promise it is worth waiting for.

In time, the seasons of our lives will begin again. We will survive the seasons of loss because we have no choice but to believe there must be a summer. A hazy, distant memory of summer is all we have to hold on to, but our loved ones promise it is waiting for us. The seasons will repeat themselves many times over the course of our lifetime, but every season we endure is one season less until we find an endless summer of joy in the hereafter. The souls know that one fine day it will happen. Until then, we walk through our seasons, but we learn to follow the sun.

7.

THE POWER
of HOPE

I was on a book tour in 1999 that took me, among other places, to the great state of Florida. My publicist told me about a reporter for a local newspaper who was very interested in an interview, but because my schedule was so hectic it would have to be done via phone. We squeezed the interview between two bookstore appearances, where I knew I would be talking about and demonstrating mediumship for the crowd, most of whom were hoping to hear from a loved one passed on. After the first stop we drove back to the hotel, and I could already feel that I was drained from the heat and the running around. Still, a promise is a promise, and I knew that I would have to find some more energy to make the interview a worthwhile experience for the reporter. Since newspaper interviews are mostly about the book and the author's life with regard to that book, I knew that at least I would only have to talk about my ability rather than demonstrate. That came as a welcome vacation in the middle of a busy day. I waited by the phone at the appointed time for the interviewer to call.

The gentleman who was to interview me called and introduced himself as the religion editor of the paper, which he told me was not actually a local daily paper, but rather a community press. Although I felt I was a bit misled by them as far as their readership was concerned, I found it interesting that the religion editor of a community press in a rather religiously conservative area was this interested in mediumship. Undaunted, I prepared myself to answer his questions. The first two questions were the usual stock and trade: when did I know I had this ability and how did my family react—answers to which I could probably now recite in my sleep, so I felt a comfortable "automatic pilot" mode set into me. It was his third statement that shook me back into focus.

"So go ahead," he said to me.

"Go ahead with . . . ?" I didn't know quite what he wanted me to explain.

"Go ahead and do it," he insisted, this time more pointedly.

"Do *what?*" I knew I was tired, but I was sure I didn't fall asleep at any point and miss his question. I was completely confused.

"Go ahead and prove that you communicate with the dead. Talk to my relatives," he barked, now obviously perturbed.

"*Prove* it?" I asked, astonished. "You are the religious editor of your paper and you want *me* to prove to you the existence of life hereafter? *No one* can prove that to you and the souls will never try." I felt embarrassed and insulted at the same time—being barked at to perform like a show pony for his apparent entertainment. Fortunately, before I said anything in anger, my tongue was stopped by the souls in the hereafter, who placed an image in my head to make me understand his perspective. Years of disappointment in his life had caused his beliefs to erode, and so he was challenging me, in essence, to help him bolster his sagging faith. I waited for a moment, and then spoke to him in the most conciliatory tone I could muster. "The souls have done many things for their loved ones here, and have sometimes talked themselves blue trying to make us understand their world. In all my years of hearing from them, I know the one thing they won't do is tamper with our beliefs or our spiritual journey here. All the communication in the world wouldn't prove their existence to you, and if that's what you came for, I'm afraid you've wasted your time." He said nothing; he just hung up. I found the irony of the situation funny and sad at the same time: this gentleman was hoping that something he didn't believe in would help restore his faith in something he did believe in. Learning to hold on to our hope and faith in what the souls, religion, or even our own instincts have taught us is probably one of the hardest of our experiences on the earth. Sometimes our hope in a better life will be all we have to see us through in difficult times, and it is this hope that we must guard with our lives—once lost, it is almost impossible to replace. That is why, after we have experienced loss on the earth, our loved ones in the hereafter reach out to us so fervently to keep the fire of hope burning within us. Many people have found that at the very time when they feel their faith and hope in danger of slipping away, they receive a sign or a visitation from a loved one passed on that plants the seed within them to keep going and keep believing. It is the souls' job in the hereafter to help us through, but they can't make things so clear to us that the challenge is no longer there. The hurdle will still be before us, but the souls can do just enough to plant that small spark to rekindle our faith.

Through scientific testing at a few of the universities who research mediumistic ability, I have been told that my accuracy during the sessions is about ninety percent. Some have often asked why, if I am hearing directly from the souls, the score is not perfect. The answer is very simple: ninety percent of their world is all the souls can tell us. I used to think that it was because of my own inability to completely understand the souls, or that there were things communicated through the sessions that were either impossible to verify or not understood by the recipient of the information. It is only as I get older that I understand that the souls can *never* give us one hundred percent. No matter how much information they communicate during the course of a discernment, they will never leave me, the researchers, or their loved ones convinced that life does *absolutely* exist for us in another dimension. The souls are very matter of fact in answering my own frustration about not knowing with absolute certainty that they are communicating from the hereafter and in telling me that if we had all the answers here on the earth, then there would be no point in going through the test. They know that they can never solve the problem for us on the earth—they can only point us in the direction of the answer, and the rest is up to us. The souls in the hereafter purposely keep that picture from becoming crystal clear to *all* of us, because it simply isn't for us to know without question—and without cultivating our own hope and belief that it *will* be there. As for me, I have no doubt that the souls exist, but as much as I have seen and heard from the hereafter, they are relentless in not having me know for sure that their world is there. It is literally for them to know, and for us, with our hope, to spend a lifetime finding out.

Belief in life eternal can be a scary thought; it means that we might actually be accountable for everything we say and do in this lifetime. I think the souls are absolutely right in leaving that part of the picture slightly fuzzy for us. Most people are not comfortable with the knowledge that an "Infinite Light" is presenting us with opportunities and struggles in all areas of our lives and relationships, and that the outcome of those opportunities and struggles will be subject to review later on. Sometimes I think humankind's greatest invention of comfort on the earth is its ability to just forget things that are upsetting or uncomfortable, or worse—to pretend they never happened. We have cultivated a sort of "spiritual amnesia" when it comes to things that we cannot or *will not* deal with. Belief in life hereafter makes us more conscious, and therefore more culpable, for our actions than we may want to be. But the souls remind us constantly through the sessions that what we do here is our opportunity to shine on the earth, and show the Infinite Light that not only are we are listening and learning, we are seizing the opportunity to grow spiritually on the earth, as we were sent here to do. What we have done in our lives will have a lasting impression on our final review of our spiritual gains when it is our time to leave the earth.

The dictionary defines *hope* as "Desire, accompanied by expectation of, or belief in, fulfillment." How stunningly accurate that meaning is when I think of the world hereafter. The reward of maintaining hope on the earth is fulfillment of what we so desperately yearn for, and what the souls tell us we are perfectly entitled to—life in the Garden of Souls. In many of the sessions I have done, the souls, in one way or another, have also added their own perspective to our world's meaning of the word. *Hope,* the souls have said, is the ability to nurture the fragile flower of our spiritual beliefs, in spite of the fact that aspects of our life here might not have an immediately clear or apparent reason; it is any time we must resign the demands of the conscious self to the patience of the spiritual self. Our conscious self *needs* answers to questions, but our spiritual self, having much greater vision, contents itself with the understanding that one day sense will be made of the senseless. There are so many of us who have fallen down in our hope because the questions are too many and the answers too few, but the souls assure us that hope can be found in those moments when we walk the most blindly through our purpose here. We are all writing the stories of our lifetime on the earth. It includes people and circumstances designed by the Infinite Light to leave us with incomplete chapters. Some are short, some painful, some tragic—others are joyous, mysterious, and fleeting. They are *all* chapters, however, that are written with the people who will become heroes, and circumstances that will be triumphs. The souls ask us to use the strength of our hope, like a marker, to underscore the great adventure of our lives here. It is the story of our journey to the Light, and they know for certain it has a happy ending.

HOPE LOST

Depending on your belief system, most people think that the first casualty in the passing of a loved one is their physical life. Because I hear the words from the souls who have passed into the hereafter and see them in all their glory—young, well, vibrant, able to walk, free of pain, and truly *happy*—I have to disagree with the belief that death means the end of life. To me, the first real casualty in the passing of a loved one is our hope—it disappears from us like water through a sieve, especially when it is most needed for us to cope. It is an unfortunate part of the work I do that I will occasionally come across someone who is so embittered by their loss that the assistance and the *hope* that can come through from their loved ones in the hereafter simply cannot reach them. They become blind and deaf to the reality that they *must* continue walking, even through their pain, if they are going to even benefit minutely from this difficult leg of the journey of their spiritual lives. Any challenge left unfaced in this lifetime is wasted, but we must make the decision to face the pain, or we subvert the rest of our lessons by turning our back to the very reason we are here—to walk, to run, to fall, to cry, to crawl, to stand up, and to walk again.

I try very hard to understand some of the people I have seen during a session who seem to have completely lost their hope. It is quite natural, and even understandable, to momentarily find yourself angry, bitter, and spiritually empty; it is an unfortunate by-product of the pain of loss. We all need time to heal and allow perspective to return. In some people, however, they allow their hopelessness to become solid and immoveable, and it will become the labor of friends, loved ones, the souls in the hereafter—and even ourselves—to chip away at that stone until the light of hope can be seen through it.

The loss of hope that follows tragedy will have to be dealt with before the more constructive process of learning to cope can ever take place. Although it may be a problem to overcome, it is at least a problem that can be seen and felt—and any problem easy to recognize will be easier to fix. What is far more destructive, however, is to come to the great wall of adversity that we all must climb after tragedy in order to continue, only to sit down in front of it and wait for it to crumble, without even trying to venture over it. Refusal to face the prospect of lost hope is a refusal to reconcile ourselves to the very circumstances we are sent here to experience and overcome.

I was in Houston, Texas, a few years ago, where I met a lovely Korean family who had come for a session. They were three generations of women—a grandmother, mother, and two daughters. One of the daughters told me that since her grandmother did not speak English and her mother had only limited knowledge of English, she would be translating as I was speaking. I assured her that it would be no problem at all, and that I would stop periodically to allow her to relay my words in Korean to her mother and grandmother. The session started rather quickly, as a young man moved forward at once to say he was the *son* and *brother* to the women there. The young woman seated there translated, and I waited for confirmation.

"No," the mother replied.

"Well, there is a young male here who states he is related to you all, so I will answer yes for you and continue," I replied, assuming they might be a little nervous and need more time to remember a young male passed on in their family. The young man continued, this time more insistently.

"This young man tells me he is the son and he is the brother passed on—to all of *you*." People might be a little nervous at the beginning of a session, but I don't think they would forget having lost a son and brother. The young woman translated, and I looked to them for acknowledgment.

"No," the mother replied again. Her other daughter leaned to her and told her something in Korean, but the mother shook her head and stated once again, "No."

Now I was confused—apparently I was missing something. I focused on the young man more carefully. There was something already a little odd about the session, I had noticed. The souls normally come in such a flurry; they are active, and sometimes communicate so much information at one time that I wind up jumbling what they wanted to say. This young man, however, seemed a little passive to me—rather like he was not going to push terribly hard to get his information across. He told me that the woman directly in front of me was his mom.

I looked at the mother. "He tells me *you* are Mom."

Her daughter translated. "Yes," she answered, smiling.

I'm not sure what I had missed the first time, but I continued. "He says he is *your* son." I found myself speaking more slowly, just in case my words were being misinterpreted.

"Yes," she answered. "My son."

Okay, I thought to myself. *Now we're cooking with gas.* I wasn't sure why they didn't understand the information the first time I told them, but we seemed to be making progress.

The young man showed me a park—not a city park, but a huge one, like Yosemite, with mountains, boulders, and ravines. He gave me the impression he had been on vacation. I told this to the family, and the young lady translated. Mother and grandmother seemed very excited at the statement. "Yes, yes," they both said, smiling with complete understanding. I continued listening to the young man, who showed me a rockslide down a ravine he had been standing near. The next image I saw was him being swept down a far distance along with the rocks. Apparently, he had lost his footing during the rockslide and fallen into the ravine.

"Your son tells me that he had fallen from some height; he's showing me he's being swept down the side of a mountain with the falling rocks." I looked to the daughter to translate, but she hesitated, as if she were unsure how to translate my words. She waited one second, and then translated for her mother. Her mother, hearing the translation, bore the look of concern.

"No, no," she told me gravely.

"That's what he's telling me. He fell from a type of mountain during a rockslide, into a type of ravine," I told her, trying to be as clear as possible. The daughter looked helpless. She started translating, but her mother cut her off in midsentence and shot back at her daughter in Korean. Then she turned back to me. "No, no, no," she said emphatically.

If her son wasn't quite so clear about the description of his passing, I might have just concluded that I had either missed something or misunderstood the images he was showing me. Then a thought came to me, and I looked to the daughter. "Maybe your mother doesn't know the manner of his passing?" I offered.

The young woman looked helpless again. "I don't think so."

Something was definitely not right. The young man in the hereafter did not seem too concerned whether his family understood or not, none of this information was making any sense to the mother, and the daughter seemed so reluctant to translate what I was saying. My mind started racing back through the session and what the young man had said and shown me, looking for any possible way that I could have completely missed something that would have made any sense to this family. I stopped, took a breath, and addressed all four women. "Something is wrong here, and I'm not sure why, so let me go back and tell you again what your son and your brother has told me up until this point." I gathered my thoughts, and listed the facts as I heard them. "Okay, this young man tells me he is your son, and brother to the young ladies. He told me about vacationing in a state park or something, and he showed me himself falling from a mountain with rocks all around him. So far does any of this make any sense to any of you?"

The daughter began translating, but I interrupted her. "And now he tells me to say to you that he was lost." The daughter continued translating, and when she finished, her mother shook her head. The mother looked at me, and in an apparent attempt to make me understand, patted her chest as she spoke in broken English.

"My son," she said, watching my face for signs of understanding.

"*Yes,*" I answered, wishing so badly that I could speak Korean this very moment. "Your son."

"Yes," she said resolutely, pleased that I was understanding her. "*Where is he?*"

Our victory over language was short-lived. "Now *I* don't understand," I told the daughter. I repeated the question to the mother. "Where *is* he?"

"*Yes,*" she stated again, in relief that I was finally getting her message. I wasn't.

"Where is his body?" I asked, confused.

The mother looked exasperated. "Where is *he*—my son?"

I have to admit I was reaching the end of my patience. We were about twenty-five minutes into the session, and it apparently had yet to start. "Where *is* he in the hereafter, like his *location?*" I looked to the daughter, who had, at this point, slumped back on the sofa in resignation. Midway through her translation, her mother cut her off, spoke to her daughter with a pointed tone, then crossed her arms and sat back, staring at the furnishings in the room.

My head was starting to hurt. I thought maybe I was just tired, that I was just not able to make a connection to this young man who I understood, but apparently no one else did. I felt humiliated, and I just wanted this session to end. "Maybe I should just stop," I told the two sisters. "For some reason none of this is making any sense to you, and I feel like I've wasted your time."

The sisters looked at each other and then at me. "No, please don't stop," one of the sisters told me. "My mother doesn't understand, but we do."

"How can that be?" I asked her. "Is it a language thing?"

"No," she answered. "It's hard to explain. Please continue."

In all the mayhem going on around me, I hadn't noticed that the line of communication was still open with the young man in the hereafter, who smiled serenely and gave me the feeling that he had somehow been vindicated. "Okay," I told them, "But just so I don't think I've gone insane, this is your brother, correct?"

Both sisters smiled at me. "Yes."

I continued with the session, not really knowing where we had left off, but terrified to even reiterate any of the information the young man told me previously. He continued on about being lost, that he is now safe and in a happy place, and that the accident was no one's fault. He told me that in spite of how the circumstance of his passing might sound or look, it was a peaceful passing, and he wasn't frightened. He wanted his sisters to know how much he cared for them, not only as siblings, but also as friends. Before he left, he warned the sisters to have patience, because there would be a struggle with their mother that may never resolve itself. The sisters nodded in understanding. He wished them well in their young lives, and congratulated one of the sisters on a promotion that was soon to happen. As he began to withdraw, he seemed almost apologetic to me. He then said, *"Make sure my mom knows I love her,"* and disappeared.

"He says to make sure his mom knows he loves her," I told the sisters. I thought to myself, *Just don't tell her until you are out of this room.*

When the session ended, the sisters rose to shake my hand. "Thank you—this was wonderful," the sister who had been translating told me. "Everything was correct."

I was incredulous. "You must be joking."

The young woman looked at her mother, who sat, staring straight ahead of her with no interest. "She doesn't understand, but we do."

The sisters explained to me that more than a year before the session, their brother vanished while on a camping trip. After weeks and then months of searches, he was presumed dead. This information was unacceptable to his mother, however, who decided that he needed time away from his family, school, and friends, and would contact them when he was ready. No matter how much her daughters argued, his mother would not allow any memorial service or acknowledgment of his passing. She had decided just to wait, until he was ready to come back. The sisters thought that the session would help bring some closure, but it was actually more difficult than they thought. They admitted that even they held out some small hope that he had just wanted to disappear from the family for a time, but when he appeared to me, they knew he was gone. The sisters thanked me once again and started toward the door with their grandmother. Their mother walked past me and out the door without looking back. I thought I would feel angry or insulted, but instead I sat down and said a little prayer for a woman who has a very, very trying journey ahead of her.

HOPE FOUND

There are some words in almost every language that have been so overused that their very meanings have been diluted, even cheapened. The true meaning of these words begin suffering from a barrage of clichés, platitudes, and expressions that make us forget how profound these words are. I am sure that no one will argue that the word *love* has all but lost its power to move people with its meaning. You *love* your children, but somehow you can also *love* a good steak, you can *love* the way that color looks on her, and also *love* to help him out, but can't—all at the very same time. I have found that the word *hope* is quickly becoming another one of those words, but I think the effect of its overuse is a lot more destructive. Overusing a word that so well demonstrates our fervent need for strength when the world has gone mad for us stops us from hearing its true meaning. It prevents us from hearing the desperation in the voices of the people who can only whisper it, when they *hope* their child was not in that wreck, they *hope* he had an opportunity to say goodbye to her before she passed, and they *hope* they can carry the pain one more day without wanting to end their own life. We don't really understand the meaning and value of our hope, until it is blown by winds of tragedy right out of our hands. Then, because we are on our hands and knees searching for it, each speck we can recover is more precious than the last.

Hope is like a diamond—strong and beautiful, but also fragile and easily damaged under the right circumstances. Hope that is damaged as a result of losses, setbacks, and failures may not be easily repaired, but opportunities to find new hope in the world around us are plentiful, if we know where to look. Hope is everywhere on the earth. But like a diamond, the only way it can be recovered is by smashing the boulders of despair that surround it. Like mining for a perfect gem of restored hope, tons of stone have to be blasted to find those small, brilliant stones scattered beneath the heavy rock.

Hope, like a rare gem, is also found in the unlikeliest of places, and requires hard work to unearth. Once found again, however, most people will not covet and tighten their grip on their newfound hope; on the contrary, they will share it with others. This generosity should not confound us who have never lost our grip on hope; it is among the most valuable of lessons that the souls in the hereafter can share with us.

I wrote about my friend Susan Marek previously in *Lessons from the Light*, when she came to see me after losing a son, Ryan, to leukemia. This was the second loss of a son for Susan, and the loss proved to be too much for her to handle. As a nurse and as a mother, Susan felt like a failure in both areas, and in the haze of her grief saw no other alternative to her pain than to consider ending her own life to be with her boys. Susan is one of those odd circumstances of intervention by the souls in the hereafter, because her sons, both named Ryan, went out of their way to have their mother come to see me. After speaking to her just the day before (the day of her son's funeral) and telling her no appointments were available where we were working in South Carolina, we suddenly had a last-minute cancellation, and not one of the families on the wait-

ing list were able to come on such short notice. In the meantime, someone had just given Sue their frequent-flyer miles as a gift so that she
could afford a plane trip. The amount of impossible coincidences, however, pales in comparison to the amount of work her boys had to do
from the hereafter to convince their mom it was imperative that she
continue on the earth.

The session did have a profound effect on Susan, and I know it did
help; she is still thriving on the earth. It has been five years since her session, but I recently had the chance to talk to her and find out how things
were going. I could find no better tribute to the power of hope than to
hear about her life since her loss. Although she still struggles with her
grief every day, Susan is now working in a hospice, helping other parents to cope with the terminal illness and eventual passing of their children. To these parents, Susan is a fountain of experience and hope,
because they can see that parents can actually survive after the loss of a
child. She is an inspiration to me, because her very life proves that her
sons were right, even if she could not understand it then; that her life is
worth living, even though it didn't look that way at the time. In sharing
her gift of hope with others, she is helping countless other grieving parents find a reason to continue living.

PASSING THE TORCH OF HOPE

I hear so many circumstances of tragedy and struggle that sometimes the
cumulative effect dampens my own hope. While the medium in me understands that it is necessary for our spiritual growth to endure painful
experiences, the human in me sometimes wonders why the lessons all
have to be so *hard*. Sometimes I begin to doubt whether my ability has
any value, since all it does is constantly point out how wonderful it is *there*

and how difficult it is *here.* I am so grateful that the Infinite Light keeps its eye on me during the times I start to fall down in my own hope, and puts me in the path of something or *someone* whose very presence and wisdom are an inspiration to me and my work. They are a beacon of light that illuminates every path they cross. This beacon of light is the torch of hope that we receive, become illuminated by, and pass again to another in need.

A few months ago, I happened to be invited to dinner in New York City by a friend of mine. I met this gentleman through a mutual friend a few years ago, around the time he was making the conversion from Protestant to Roman Catholic. At the time, he told me about a wonderful priest who was such an inspiration to him throughout the process of converting to Catholicism, and his hope that one day I would be able to meet him. Although he knew that my work was not recognized by the Catholic Church, he knew that this priest would be able to see past the methods I use to understand the value of restoring hope and peace to the bereaved, no matter how it was achieved. As it turned out, on the evening we were to have dinner, my friend was on his way to drop off some papers to this priest, and asked if I wouldn't mind accompanying him. I agreed, and we made our way up the avenue to visit the priest who had made such an impact on my friend's life.

The priest was a kind, gentle man of great wisdom and spirituality. He also possessed an impressively immense knowledge of the spiritual practices of many cultures, from the dawn of time to New Age—including the practice of mediumship. After being introduced, I was surprised to learn that he had actually read about my work, and was intrigued by the references to the saints who appear in the sessions, as well as what they represented. Although the Catholic Church's official position on mediumship is that it cannot condone the practice, many in the Church can still find some measure of value in any earnest effort to bring comfort, hope, and a belief in life hereafter to the bereaved. The priest seemed especially interested in a session I had, where the Virgin Mary, mother of Jesus and herself a bereaved mother, appeared to comfort a woman who had also lost her son. While the method of her appearance (through mediumship) was not within the Church's beliefs, we did find common ground on how important it was for people to see the saints as human—just like us, but whose spiritual perfection when they were on the earth made them vessels of the Infinite Light. We talked about how just knowing that they were also human helps all who struggle to know what is possible through the miracle of hope. He told me an incredible story that happened when he was a young priest that helped him understand in a real way how miracles of hope happen before us every day.

One day, the young priest received a call about an emergency. The call came on Good Friday, the day when Roman Catholics around the world mourn the death of Christ. He had been alerted that a young boy had been struck by a car while riding his bicycle, and that because of his grave injuries, it might be necessary to perform the last rites. He rushed to the scene of the accident, and found the boy lying in the street and the boy's mother kneeling beside him, screaming. The paramedics worked quickly to place the boy on a gurney and transport him to the hospital, and the priest rode in the ambulance with the boy and his mother to the hospital. Looking down at the boy, his heart sank; the boy had been very badly injured and might not survive much longer. As the ambulance weaved through the New York streets, it became evident that the boy was dying.

By the time they reached the hospital, the boy had already died. Seeing the expression on the paramedics' faces, his mother became hysterical. She pulled her son into her arms and carried him through the emergency room doors. Doctors and nurses knew there was nothing more they could do. His mother stood there, inconsolable, clutching her dead son in her arms and screaming. For this priest and the others, it was a terrifying sight. No one knew what could possibly be said at this moment to bring any comfort to a mother who had just watched her son's precious life slip away. A nurse slowly walked over to the mother and helped her gently lower the boy onto a stretcher. "Another woman lost her son today," the nurse said quietly. "Her name was Mary, and her son's name was Jesus. You are not alone in your pain."

On the way home that evening, I thought about the story the priest told me. He said that he would never forget that day, or the hope those simple words brought him, as long as he lived. I wondered about the nurse, and if she knew what a profound gift she gave that bereaved mother. I thanked him for the story, because a story of hope is a gift that keeps on giving, and also is a perfect example of how the hereafter creates a lifeline of hope within reach of all of us to grab hold of when we need to. It is amazing, when you consider that this particular lifeline went from a nurse, to a mother, to a priest, to me, and to you. Hope, like the Infinite Light, is eternal.

I am very fortunate that I never have to look very far for examples in life that teach me the power of the Infinite Light on earth. The souls, in their continual quest to bring their wisdom to others in a way even I can understand, will always set a remarkable circumstance in front of me so I can learn from it and pass this gift of knowledge to others. Sometimes the examples come in the form of people I meet or the places I go, but all of it is designed for one purpose: to receive, and then pass to another the torch of hope.

THE PATTERSONS

If there is a "Big Book of Past Lives" when I finally graduate to the here-after, I would look into it, if only just to confirm my suspicion that I have been friends for many lifetimes with Pauline and Dennis Patterson. I say that, because my horrible shyness usually prevents me from feeling comfortable with people when I first meet them. But when I met Pauline and Denny, the ease and comfort I felt with them gave me a sense of déjà vu that I naturally assume is the result of having known them in a previous incarnation. It is either that, or my second theory, which I know as fact: they are truly extraordinary people.

I met Pauline and Denny when they came from Washington State, hoping to hear something from their son Jeffrey, who had been passed on five years. Although most people seek the opportunity to make communication within the first frantic year of their loss, Pauline and Denny had their family, friends, and their faith to see them through this painful time in their lives. Time heals all wounds, they knew, but time was not healing this one. Pauline, with her strong convictions and faith, found herself unable to reconcile her grief to God's will, and as birthdays, anniversaries, and milestones passed without their son, both Pauline and Denny found themselves less and less able to cope with the unanswered questions, the unacceptable answers, and the maze of self-doubt about having made the right decisions concerning their son's care.

Pauline could recall the day and the hour in June 1984, when she first sensed that something was wrong with her son Jeff. Mothers just have that special ability. She noticed that her son, who was coaching Little League baseball at the time, was losing weight. She also noticed that there was some bruising and lumps on his neck. Their family doctor was not available at the time, so they brought Jeff to the attending doctor.

This doctor surmised that it could be, at worst, a case of mononucleosis, and at best, Overprotective Mom Syndrome. He sent them home. Two weeks later, Jeff's condition worsened, and he became so weak that he could not walk without help. When Pauline and Denny brought him back a second time, their family doctor had returned and took his condition seriously enough to order a blood workup. The results soon after stunned them: Jeff had leukemia.

Acute lymphoblastic leukemia, or ALL, is rare in young adults; Jeff should have been well out of the age range for this childhood disease. It was a statistical improbability, yet Jeff was ill. He was sent to an oncologist at the hospital, who made arrangements for Jeff to receive chemotherapy immediately. The whole situation was beginning to take on the aura of the surreal for the Pattersons; they arrived at the hospital to find that the bed Jeff was assigned was in a pediatric oncology ward—the doctor not realizing that Jeff was already grown. Denny recalled to me how funny it would have been if it weren't so tragic—his son, a young man—in a tiny bed, surrounded by children, toys, and balloons. Although it was a frightening and difficult series of days, weeks, and then months, his first protocol of chemotherapy seemed to work; Jeff had gone into remission.

Although Jeff's treatment extended into the beginning of his senior year at high school, he was tutored until he was able to join his class later that year and graduate. Life returned to a reasonable facsimile of normal now that Jeff was well, and Pauline and Denny returned to their home-building project. Happily, their only concern now was figuring out why the well on their new property ran out of water every summer.

There is a point in every life when something will happen to us, and we know life will never be the same again for us. That moment came for the Pattersons in September of 1987—Jeff's third year at Eastern University—when he discovered a lump in his testicle. He was immediately placed in a one-hundred-day chemotherapy protocol to prepare him for a bone marrow transplant—a procedure that was his only chance for survival. On February 16, in a medical center in Seattle, Jeff, Denny, and Pauline placed their hope in the small bag of bone marrow plasma that was to alter the course of their lives.

The procedure was successful, but the result was disheartening. Ten days after the transplant, Jeff's white cell count began plummeting and the bone marrow was being rejected by his body. The condition, called graft-versus-host, caused his kidneys to shut down and his body to react defensively to the invasion of the foreign matter. Rather than bolster the body's defenses against disease, the transplant now caused the reverse—his body was disintegrating at an alarming pace.

No parent should ever have to live with the image of their children in agony, and no parent ever completely lives again after seeing it. Even so many years after his passing, Pauline and Denny could only finish telling me the story of their son's brutal fight in voices that had diminished to an emotional, halted whisper. Skin is a major organ of the body, and as the organs of the body falter, the skin also breaks down. Jeff's skin had begun to disintegrate on his body, leaving the kind of open wounds associated with victims of severe burns. His skin was being eaten away so quickly that a specialist had to be called in to replace his damaged skin with layers of pigskin. There is incredible, constant pain involved, because the nerves under the skin are now exposed. Denny is still haunted by the memory of his son screaming as he tried to hold him down while the skin patches were applied. In the end, none of the efforts they exhausted could turn the path away from its destination. On April 12, 1988, at three o'clock in the afternoon, Jeffrey Patterson passed quietly to a world of peace.

I never really knew the whole story of Jeff's battle until a few years after the time the Pattersons first came for a session. At that time, they were very much like the majority of bereaved parents I see—plagued with doubts about having done the right thing, angry at God for their child's suffering, hoping that their child would communicate, and skeptical that some guy on Long Island could facilitate that happening. They told me afterward that the session brought them such comfort; Jeff spoke about the value of this as a spiritual lesson for both himself and them, and spoke about ongoing family issues, which helped them understand he was still part of the family—even the well and the water problems. Things, Jeff told us, had indeed returned to normal in his new life.

I got to see Pauline and Denny many times after that whenever I visited Spokane. It always gladdened me to see how well they were doing each time I went there; they were positive, upbeat, and dealing well with their loss. The Pattersons are recovering, I used to think—they are doing just fine.

We on the earth have our spiritual flaws, but I think that the one flaw that must irritate our loved ones in the hereafter most would be our relentless ability to get suckered into complacence. If the fire alarm does not go off, we have no reason to assume there is a fire. In my own work, it is so easy to assume that if someone has not fallen apart because of their loss, they are doing well. Maybe we don't really *want* to know, but the souls know we *have* to know.

It was easy for me to lull myself into that kind of complacency watching Pauline and Denny work with the bereaved families, who would come to the sessions when I would work in Spokane. Sponsoring the sessions was not an easy task, emotionally; they not only had to work with people in grief, but they also had to open the wounds of their own tragedy when they talked to others about it. They bore it extremely well, however, and these two upbeat and energetic people arranged things so wonderfully, it appeared to have been very easy for them. One day, after a session, I happened to be sitting in the hotel lobby when Denny surprised me by showing up during his lunch hour. We laughed about my sitting in the lobby by myself like a little lost boy, and he gave me an update on a family he knew who had come to see me the day before. They were grateful for the opportunity, he told me, and the session had brought them much-needed comfort. They also lost a son to a terminal illness, so their session was of particular interest in Denny. Hearing that, I glibly went on about how the souls tell us how everything is a challenge, and everything has a reason, no matter what the outcome, but Denny stopped me midsentence.

"Well, I guess I'll believe that when I see it," he said, smirking. I was a little surprised at the tone in his words, thinking maybe that he had not really understood me. I reminded him that even his son Jeff had made a point of telling him in his own session that his suffering had a purpose in helping him to his completion on the earth, but as I continued, I watched Denny's expression grow dark.

"Well, I'm sure he said it, but I still won't understand it," he told me flatly, trying hard to remain polite, but not quite able to veil the acrimony in his voice. I realized that what I was saying upset him, and I thought this might be a good time to put my sock in my mouth, since my foot was already there. I had never seen Denny any way else but positive and open-minded. I felt foolish that up until now, even after his son's communication during the session, I had never really thought of the Pattersons as bereaved—as if good cheer and willingness to help others could in any way neutralize the pain of losing their son. But in that instant, I realized that no matter how articulate or well mannered, loss of a loved one is an open tear in the vessel of our hope, and it is only through constant vigilance that we keep it all from going empty.

I felt bad about upsetting Denny, but I continued in spite of myself. I *had* to. I knew it was more important than ever to reiterate what his own son had told me in his session and many like it, no matter how difficult it was to hear. I spoke slowly and quietly this time, telling him that one fine day, he will find himself in the completion of his work here, and would see his son again in the Garden of Souls; that Jeff would sit him down, congratulate him on his accomplishment, and tell him at long last *why* it had to happen. I told Denny that after hearing this, with no pain in his heart, and such joy in reunion, he will say the words he has waited a lifetime to say, "Ah, *now* I understand—*that's* what it was all about." And better than that, with his son at his side, what happened in that terrible time no longer matters. I looked up to find a completely unexpected reaction: Denny's eyes had welled up with tears.

Our struggle is a tornado, where the shrill siren shatters the ears with *why, why, why*. It circles relentlessly—so much so that those beaten by a storm that will not pass cannot always remember when the sky was blue. The thought of actually seeing a blue sky again is almost overwhelming when the storm will not pass. The souls need our help sometimes, because their power to help us is diminished if their presence is overlooked. It is part of our work in this lifetime, no matter what our own obstacles, to assist in the lifeline of hope. In what we do and who we are, we can become a lifeline strong enough for others to hang on to. The more hands in the chain of hope, the stronger it becomes for each of us.

I think back to the story that Pauline and Denny told me about their son Brian. I had been at their house for dinner with their two sons, Brian and Greg. During the conversation, while we were talking about the antics of the Patterson boys as young men, Pauline told me that Brian had been the bone marrow donor for his brother Jeff. Not only did he endure the painful procedure to help his brother, but he underwent the procedure a *second* time, because his bone marrow was a match for another young man who desperately needed it. Pauline beamed and told me how proud she was of Brian, who could only shrug his shoulders and blush at the attention. Brian's story illustrates what the souls say about our hope defying all human terms, like logic, emotion, and thought. I asked Pauline and Denny if they believed at the time that the bone marrow would save their son's life. They told me that although they hoped for a miracle, they knew that at best it could only buy him some more time. That is what hope *does*; it realigns our vision to allow us to see what may be impossible, but to accept what likely is probable. But what I found more fascinating than that is the fact that Brian chose to undergo a second bone marrow procedure—the day before his own brother's funeral. I wondered why, after undergoing such a painful procedure only to have it produce no real result, would he even bother to undergo it again, this time for a stranger, knowing that this stranger was no more likely to survive than his brother. Pauline asked me if I wanted an answer to my question from Brian. I didn't need one—the souls answered for him. That is what hope *is*. It is that tiny window, between doubt and despair, that the Infinite Light can burst its lustrous rays through to touch our hearts. I think about Pauline, Denny, and the boys often, and sometimes even see Jeff in the corner of my thoughts. I think about their incredible gifts of hope to me and to others, and I say often in the quiet of my heart, "Hang on, Pattersons—hang on."

Early on in my career as a medium, I found myself without any concrete answers to give people when they asked the fundamental questions about the importance of loss in our experiences on the earth, and the value of hope to our spiritual growth here. I heard what the souls were saying, but I found it difficult to crystallize the true meaning of their messages. I could tell people what I *believed* the point of their communication was, but until I was shown, directly, through the example of the souls communicating, the best I could do was guess at the larger picture the souls were trying to show all of us who heard their communication. I repeatedly asked the souls to help me understand what *message* they were trying to convey in the course of communication to their loved ones here, and quite fortunately for me, I did not have to wait very long for an answer.

I had an incredible dream one night. I found myself walking in a place I had never seen before, through a forest of such beauty I could never describe it. Everything around me was filled with undulating energy—the grass, the rocks, the flowers, the trees—and the sense of love I felt was so palpable it was as if I could hold it in my hands and release it again into the sky. I felt so exhilarated by the joy that filled everything around me, that I found it impossible to stand still. I wanted to run, and to jump, or perhaps, even to fly. I continued walking, past beautiful hills under a vibrant sky, and in looking at the magnificence of this place, I began to understand where I was. I was walking in the Garden of Souls.

I came upon a place by a lake where brilliantly colored fish swam among tall golden reeds, and there I saw the figure of a man I knew well. He sat on a rock, watching the sun cascade like diamonds across the surface of the clear, velvety water. I sat down next to him, sensing his love for me, and feeling his happiness at finding me here. I knew this man well, and he knew me. It was St. Anthony, who many on the earth consider the patron of things lost. His kind face smiled as he looked upon the water, and his robes were tiny billions of stars that came together to make a cloth. He didn't turn to face me, or even speak aloud, but I heard every thought that came from his heart, and it registered in perfect sequence in mine:

> *Hope is like a golden ring. If I took the ring from your finger and tossed it into a lake, you would not have it, and it would be gone forever. If I took the ring from your finger, and held it in the palm of my hand forever, you also would not have*

it, but it would never be lost. This is hope; knowing that what we hold precious is held in the hand of the Infinite Light—forever.

That is the very nature of our hope on earth—knowing the things taken from us on the earth will be returned one fine day in the Garden of Souls. In the meantime, we can only continue in the trust that our loved ones are in very good care until they return to us.

8.

THE GIFT— HOW *the* SOULS HELP REMAKE OUR LIVES AFTER TRAGEDY

One thing I have learned after so many years of listening to the souls in the hereafter is that there is no challenge, no struggle, no tragedy, and no burden given to us by the Infinite Light that is too much for us to bear. Our experiences on the earth are chosen carefully in order to test the limits of our faith, hope, and endurance in order to fully accomplish what we have been sent to the earth to do. We have not been thrown to the earth to face our struggles unarmed; the Infinite Light will supply us with the means we will need not only to survive tragedy, but to grow again and flower in the face of despair. It is called The Gift—the extraordinary perception we are given to see past the confines of the small world we lived in prior to tragedy. Ask anyone who has endured any type of loss—loss of a loved one, loss of a job, or even the loss of the ability to make sense of their own lives—and they will recount for you the remarkable and life-changing things that seem to have just *happened* around them to assure them that they are not fighting the battle alone. The Infinite Light knows that we do not have the capability to understand why loss and change are so necessary to fulfilling our destiny on the earth. Rather than allow us to hopelessly spin our wheels, unable to move from tragedy, the souls in the hereafter reach in and try to infuse us with just a glimmer of their newfound understanding about the way of the universe and things to come. It is that tiny, almost imperceptible ray of the Infinite Light, sent to us by those who care, that we somehow instinctively know to follow out of our darkest time. It is the only consolation our loved ones can give us when so much has been taken from us, but it is given to us as a promise that *all* will be returned to us when we have concluded our journey on the earth and return to the hereafter.

The Gift is a sudden moment of clarity in the depth of grief; an understanding that perhaps this may *not* be the end of the world, no matter how dark things look, and no matter how much hope we have lost. Suddenly, and quite coincidentally, signs begin appearing everywhere for us, and our loved ones spare no expense in illustrating for us that we have never been alone in our struggle or forgotten by the Infinite Light. Impossible circumstances of beauty and hope may fall out of the sky like a sun shower, a sudden moment of joy may fill the heart, or a special person can be moved into our path to make the road a little easier. They happen with such frequency, especially just before and just after loss, they tend to make the term *coincidence* seem ridiculous. We can never control how the Gift is sent, and our loved ones cannot make us comprehend and take note of it, but it is given in the hope that we will understand and use this gift to remake the rest of our lives here and continue in faith. Like all gifts, it is the intention of the hereafter that it will be received, but it is their hope that it will be shared.

Since the hereafter has entrusted me with the responsibility of being an instrument of the souls on the earth, my entire life has been like a conduit through which the souls can deliver some of these gifts to their loved ones on the earth. What generally happens is that the souls will place me in the lesson they need me to understand, and in turn, I teach others I come into contact with. Each lesson, the painfully difficult as well as the wonderfully joyous, brings with it a story *that must be told* about the wisdom and power of the souls in the hereafter. It also creates the example others can follow and model in their own lives. I am not the only person on earth that the souls entrust with this responsibility, though; each of us, no matter what we do or who we are, will become the keeper of the story that must be told to anyone who will listen and needs to learn. In the process, the energy we give to the people we impact with the sharing of tragic circumstances on the earth will be returned to us in the form of solace and consolation. It is hard to think of tragedy and loss as a gift, but when we come to understand that *nothing* in our lifetime happens without a reason, we will one day come to understand that just the smallest sharing of what is to come, given so thoughtfully by the souls of our loved ones and the Infinite Light, is perhaps the greatest gift we will ever receive while we remain on the earth.

Anyone who knows me or has come to me for a session knows how adamant I am about not knowing any information about the person or family attending a session. I have even disqualified from coming people who have inadvertently told me who they were or whom they were hoping to make communication with. They must be anonymous at the time of their appointment, or I will feel that the communication will not have been generated solely by the hereafter. As silly as it seems, the souls still have to convince *me* that they are communicating. Many people have come to me for a session using a false name. They are so pleased afterward to know in their heart that they were indeed anonymous during the session, and the information that came across during the session could have come *only* from their loved one. That is the way I like to feel about every appointment. When the requests for appointments are received, they are assigned a number. Their name and address are sent to another office to be logged for the appointment. This system, developed over years of wanting to maintain absolute purity of the discerning process, has served us very well. Except when we need to contact someone who has come for an appointment. Then the arduous process has to go in reverse and we have to hope the information can be reassembled. It has only happened rarely that we felt the need to contact someone after an appointment, but the reason becomes quite clear afterward, and is generally motivated by the souls in the hereafter who most certainly have a plan cooking.

I don't really remember the first time I met Rosemary and Luther Smith, but I can tell you that the circumstance of having met them is not easily forgotten. One morning, on a day we had private sessions booked, I met my co-author and program director, Andrew, for breakfast. While we were finishing our coffee and talking about this and that, I felt myself pulling away from the conversation and tuning into the voices that materialized as if right behind me. It was the souls speaking—the voices of two young men, talking about who was going to speak first during their session. The sessions weren't for another few hours, but I tuned in to their conversation. They were brothers, killed in an automobile accident, and they were so excited for the opportunity to speak to their folks, who they knew needed desperately to hear that their sons made the transition and that they are happy in the hereafter. After a few seconds, I was pulled back to this world and back to my coffee, to find Andrew staring at me. "George, you haven't heard one word I've said," he chided. "What's going on?"

"Two boys are fighting in my head about who's going to talk first later," I told him, laughing at the scenario they were displaying for me.

"Which appointment do they belong to?"

I tried to tune into them again, hoping they would save me some time during their parents' appointment by getting some of the facts out of the way now, since they now had my attention. I listened carefully, and their answer was startlingly candid and funny. "*Smart-asses*," I laughed. "They're telling me to *keep my shirt on* until their parents get here." I like it when the souls come across so boisterously, because it really helps to illustrate that they are, in fact, very much alive, and continuing in the hereafter just as they were on the earth.

In one of the appointments scheduled that day, my assistant brought in a very well-dressed and charming couple who seated themselves in front of me and waited for me to begin. After a brief introduction, I launched into the session. The first image I was met with was the two boys. "Remember us?" they joked. After the session, the parents thanked me politely and left, and I remember thinking to myself that I liked them instantly because of their two boys. I don't recall them actually introducing themselves by name, but the circumstance of their good-natured and outgoing sons stayed in my memory.

Months later, a family came to a session, and afterward mentioned that they were friends of the Smiths, who made it possible for them to come by funding the appointment. I told them that I was very glad to hear that, but couldn't recall the Smiths. She pressed on by saying, "You know, Rosemary and Luther Smith." I remember thinking in my head that she must be kidding—with all the appointments I do, and with a name as common as Smith (if it was even their real name), it was impossible for me to remember them. Later on that evening, I thought about how nice it was for the "Smiths" to make a session possible for another family. That kind of sharing is what we are all about in our journey here—using our own circumstances to make the road easier for someone else.

The "Smiths" cropped up again on another occasion when I was speaking to my friend Elaine Stillwell, who mentioned this rather dynamic couple and the efforts they have made to start up grief programs in their area in order to help other bereaved parents cope with the loss of their children. It came to be that somehow or another, someone was always mentioning this couple and the wonderful things they were doing for others in pain. It made me wish I knew who they were, but I had the feeling we would see each other again.

A few months later, I was invited to speak at a Grief Support Seminar in Louisville, Kentucky, hosted by Sharon and Frank Smith (no relation, but you see what I mean about the name Smith) who themselves were bereaved parents, having lost their only daughter, Frannie, in a skiing accident in 1993. I had come to Louisville a few days earlier at the insistence of Frank Smith, because there were so many bereaved parents in need who wanted so much to hear something from their children. We agreed to set aside three days before the seminar for private sessions to help with the grieving process of some of these parents. After one of the appointments on the first day, a family whose session I had just completed told me how grateful they were for the appointment, and how grateful they were to Rosemary and Luther Smith for creating the opportunity for them to come by providing the funds to attend the session. There was that name again—now I was intrigued. So much kindness out of one couple—I told the woman I would very much like to meet them one day. "You will," she told me. "They'll be here this week." I asked her not to say any more because I cannot know who is attending which appointment, and would hate to have to disqualify a couple that has done so much good for so many. I concluded that I would have to leave it in the hands of fate to have the Smiths pointed out to me somewhere during the next ten appointments. After the day's appointments, I told my assistant about what I had heard regarding what the Smiths had done, and mentioned my interest in meeting them and thanking them for their kindness. He told me that it was difficult to know because there were three Smith families set to attend appointments while we were in Kentucky. So I did the only thing I could think of: I asked the loved ones of the Smiths to help point them out during the session if they could.

The next day I had five sessions scheduled. At the third session, my assistant escorted a well-mannered and very polite couple who said hello, thanked me for coming to Kentucky, and seated themselves. There was something vaguely familiar about them, but I wasn't sure why. I sat down and we began the session. During the session, the souls who communicated were two boys, who passed on in an automobile accident, as well as the woman's mother, who passed on from cancer. During the session I couldn't help but feel I had talked to these boys before, but they came through with so much to say that there was little time for me to think about when I could have heard from them before. When the session ended, the couple thanked me and began to rise as the door opened and my assistant came in. "George," he said, "these are the Smiths—*Rosemary and Luther.*" All at once the session made sense to me. These were the boys who joked with me before their parents came to the first session. My surprise at having met them and wanting to thank them for all their good work unfortunately gave way to a wave of shyness and self-consciousness, and all I could burble out was, "Uh, nice to meet you." When they left the room, I got my composure back and immediately called the lobby to find my assistant. "Tell them how grateful we are for their kindness, and be sure to tell them how much their generosity is appreciated by me *and* the hereafter," I barked, annoyed at myself for blowing the opportunity to tell them personally, all because of my ridiculous shyness.

It wasn't until just a year or so ago that we were able to see each other again. Rosemary found out that our book tour for *Lessons from the Light* was bringing us to Lexington, Kentucky, and she called Andrew to find out if it was possible for us to meet there. I jumped at the opportunity to invite them to have dinner with us after the book signing. Through periodic correspondence and speaking with Elaine Stillwell, I heard about the extraordinary things the Smiths were doing in the name of their boys and the souls of children everywhere, including the commission of a mural in the dome of the Inn at Cumberland College in Kentucky, and a book written by Rosemary, called *Children of the Dome*, which tells the story of twenty-eight families dealing with the loss of children. I looked forward to dinner that night, not only because of my fondness for Rosemary and Luther, but because there was an insistent feeling that the souls yet again had something up their sleeves—some circumstance they needed me to experience in order to understand more about the things they felt we on the earth needed to know. I've learned over the years not to ask how or why when the souls want to illustrate their point; following their advice has always proved beneficial, not only to me, but most important, to my work. I looked forward to not only a good learning experience, but a nice meal, with great people to boot.

The day was a very long one in Lexington, with two television programs, an interview, a luncheon at the bookstore in my honor, another interview, two radio shows, and then back to the bookstore, where more than two hundred people showed up to hear about life in the hereafter, and possibly hear directly from their loved ones. There were many souls who needed to reach loved ones in the audience that night, and there were many books that needed to be signed, so the evening went on much longer than I had originally thought. By the time things quieted down and I was able to catch my breath, I found myself suddenly exhausted by the day, and wondered if I was going to be able to make it through dinner without collapsing. Again I heard that insistent voice from the hereafter telling me to go on, and at just that point I made eye contact with Rosemary and Luther, and started to feel invigorated, and also very hungry. We said hello and made our way to the car as we talked since it was getting late and the restaurant would not be open much longer.

As Luther drove, we managed to get caught up on things that were going on in everyone's life—our book, Rosemary's book, their plans to come to New York again, and friends we had in common. The lively conversation in the car helped to give me a second wind, and I started to feel refreshed. As we approached the restaurant, we came upon a parking lot. As Luther slowed down to find a spot, we passed a small red convertible parked in a stall. Luther pointed the car out and said, "Look, that's the kind of car our boys were killed in." The simplicity of his tone to such a strong statement made me look up in the direction of the car, and suddenly I was hit by a feeling that very rarely happens—a moment of heartsickness so profound that I couldn't speak. It was as if the hereafter wanted me to understand for one second the unending pain that will be with the Smiths all of their life, no matter how happy and contented they may appear on the outside. It was a moving experience that shook me to my foundation, and one I will probably never forget. I understood all at once by that simple statement that no wealth, privilege, or good works can ever erase the pain of loss, and I felt myself momentarily living the grief of these two wonderful people who lost two precious boys, yet carry the pain with dignity and determination to maybe make someone else's life a little easier by the great things they have done.

Once inside the restaurant, I was glad the Smiths were the type of easygoing and casual people they were, as I threw manners to the wind, inhaling food and talking with my mouth full. We were having a wonderful time, talking about everything under the sun and eating the gigantic cuts of beef Kentucky is famous for. By the time dessert came, I noticed that we were the only people left in the restaurant. Rosemary talked about the session they had in Louisville, and thanked me for having made such an impact on their grieving process. I finally had the chance to thank them for all the wonderful things they have done for others, and reminded them that it has not gone unnoticed by me, their loved ones, or the hereafter, and they are blessed for having done such good in the face of such tragedy. Rosemary began to tell me that in strange way, the loss of her sons was a gift—a way for them to fulfill the purpose they now know they were sent here for. Although they will never forget their boys, the experience of helping others to understand their loss makes them feel that their boys had also fulfilled their purpose on the earth. And the gifts of love and compassion they have received in return has made their own loss more bearable. They credit their sons for giving them the gift of strength to go on, and to do as much as they can to make the load a little lighter for the next family devastated by loss. As I looked up to face them, I noticed a glow around both Rosemary and Luther—and behind them, those two beautiful, laughing boys, so proud of their parents for understanding and accepting The Gift, and sharing it with whomever should need it. It was an evening I won't soon forget.

A GIFT WHICH COMES IN MANY SHAPES AND SIZES

I have been told many times by the souls in the hereafter that when we experience the loss of a loved one, part of the profound change that comes over us is our link to a world we have never experienced, much less thought about. But the link to our loved ones can never be broken, not even in physical death, and it connects us to a world we now feel and can be affected by. The gifts of perception that we receive from the hereafter are not always conscious—we may not know or even feel that they are happening, but our loved ones assure us that the gifts come as they are needed. These gifts are sent to us not only at the time of our loss and thereafter, but sometimes they are sent as a way of preparing us to deal with grief when the loss of a loved one is immi- nent. Each of us has many souls in the hereafter, whether we recognize them or not, who are working to help us to carry out the plan that is to be our life's work on the earth. And though we might not recognize it right away, the tools we need to survive, both before *and* after tragedy, are sent to us by those souls who truly care for our well-being.

I have heard so many stories from families who have had premoni- tions about the passing of their loved ones, sometimes days, weeks, or even years before the tragedy. Mostly, they are shaken off by them as bad dreams, paranoia, or even silly nonsense. But the effects of them linger oddly in their minds, no matter how much they try to shake them. I have heard many times, as I'm sure you have, the stories of people who, im- mediately following the loss of a loved one, recall in vivid detail exactly how they were warned about an upcoming tragedy. What is tragic about these circumstances is that so many people riddle themselves with guilt, thinking that the signs were somehow given to them in order to stop a tragedy from happening. My mail is filled with letters from distraught people who feel as if they should have or could have done something to stop the inevitable simply because they felt the "notification" of im- pending loss in a sign or a dream. Other times, brokenhearted family members will tell me that very near to the end of their life here, their loved ones forecasted their passing in a cryptic way that only after their passing seemed as plain as day. But these premonitions are not intended to compound our grief after we recall them. We cannot change the life plan of any of our loved ones any more than we can change our own. The souls tell me that sometimes their passing was forecasted in an effort to help their remaining loved ones to prepare at least psychologically for the loss, and in no way to prevent it from happening. We, in our inexperience and lack of real knowledge, actually think we are in control of these things. Our loved ones passed on assure us, as delicately as they can, that we are not. The Infinite Light, sensing in its magnificent way those who might be irreparably damaged by the pain of loss, seems to leak the information in small, barely noticeable doses, to prepare us for what might very well be the shock of our lives. Our loved ones who have passed before us completely understand the fragile nature of our human spirit here, and in their compassion will try to "break it to us gently" in order to keep loss from completely destroying us in our journey here.

I was surprised to find in a session I had with a woman whose husband passed on from a terminal illness that not only was the illness a life lesson for the person about to pass, it was also a way for their loved ones here to cope in small increments with the prospect of eventually losing someone they love to physical death. As the souls always say, we are not only a teacher in any life lesson, we are also the student. Although it may be hard initially to understand that these are magnificent and valuable gifts given to us by the hereafter to help us ease into the pain of loss, our very ability to continue after loss is a testament to how well these gifts have served us.

Sometimes the gifts our loved ones give us to help us understand that we are on the correct path after loss come in the form of physical, tangible things that might be cast off as incredible coincidences had they not had such a profound effect on those who witness them. Rosemary Smith recounted in *Children of the Dome* that even before the passing of her two boys, Drew and Jeremiah, the appearance of butterflies was the way her loved ones in the hereafter helped her to comprehend and accept the bond with the hereafter we receive as a gift from our loved ones passed on:

Yellow butterflies have always been very special to me. The connection began as I stood at my mother's grave over ten years ago, four years before the boys died. My visits were infrequent because my mother is buried about seventy miles away from our home, at a small country church yard in Wolf Creek, Kentucky. My emotions had spilled over with sorrow that day. My mother was only fifty-three when she succumbed to the breast cancer she had fought for six years. Her death was so devastating to me because we had always been very close. As her only daughter, I considered her my best friend and confidante. I felt her death was the most sorrow I could bear. That proved not to be the case. Anyway, that one particular day, as I stood at her grave, I felt so alone. Suddenly, a huge yellow butterfly started circling around my head. It would not go away. I realized that the spirit of my Mom was with me. I felt more comfort than I ever had in the years since her death.

I never told anyone about this experience with the yellow butterfly. Many other times over the years, I would see a yellow butterfly in times of trouble. Still, I told no one. The afternoon of July 23rd, 1992, the day of the boys' accident, I managed to walk out our front door and try and grab a few moments to myself. As I walked down our walk, three yellow butterflies surrounded me. The joy I felt was indescribable. The significance of the three butterflies was not lost on me, even though I was in such horrible shape mentally. Well, again I did not mention this to anyone. Later, as we walked the farm looking for a burial site, three yellow butterflies kept circling around me. Finally, one of my brothers commented on it, and I told him my story. I don't know what everyone, including Luther, thought that day, but I knew that this was a powerful message from our sons who had joined my mother. The story continued as we drove behind the hearses the day of the funeral. Everyone in the car knew the story by then, so we began counting the butterflies. When we passed one hundred, we stopped counting. Many times, two yellow butterflies would come from each side of the hearse in front of us and merge, side by side, to come directly at our car. Their presence made the most difficult ride of my life bearable.

As I stated in the beginning of this chapter, the gifts we are sent come in many different shapes and sizes. Some may be large and tangible, like yellow butterflies, and others could be as small as a scent of a loved one or just the whisper of a sound that brings back the memory of a loved one's voice or speech pattern. No matter what the size or perception, they are equally valuable as proof that our loved ones are working with us from their unique place in the hereafter to help us understand our purpose for having to go through life-changing circumstances on our road here. The signs, no matter how small or seemingly insignificant to anyone else but the receiver, are sent with the same amount of love and care by souls who are concerned for our well-being and want us to carry on.

I have had many people ask me why, no matter what they do and no matter how hard they pray, they have not been given the gift of consolation in the form of a sign from their loved one. The answer is very simple: they *have* received the gift, and are continuing to receive the hope and peace of their loved ones in the hereafter as many times as they are needed in order for us to stay focused on our purpose here. I often tell people the story of my dreams of St. Catherine Labouré, who seems to visit me in my sleep with increasing frequency as I get older. The dream is always the same. She appears in her habit, surrounded in a soft blue light, and sits with me as she tells me the things she needs me to hear. Although I know she is speaking, I cannot consciously hear or understand the words, even though in my heart the words are registering and I feel the emotions and sense of understanding appropriate to what she is saying. The words are being placed in my soul in an effort to help me continue on my path here. Regardless of my actually hearing the words, I know that the effect of her wisdom has already taken root in me. I have gradually seen my perception of people and circumstances change for the better, and I feel as if somehow these words are the occasional "pep-talk" I need to stay focused in my journey here. It is apparently not important that I actually hear the words, as long as they have their intended effect in my life.

It is very much the same with the majority of people who think they have not received any signs of consolation since the passing of their loved ones into the hereafter. It is something I never fully understood until not too long ago. In many sessions, the souls will communicate to their loved ones here that they have appeared to them many times in dreams. The person in front of me will shake their head "no," but the souls will insist that they are certainly there, and appearing for our benefit to help us carry on here. I won't fight with the souls because they are never wrong, so I used to just dismiss it by saying, "I can't recall every dream I've had either." How naive we sometimes are—we live in such a physical world that we can't even comprehend the possibility of something that cannot be seen or heard, but which can still be felt. These same people who insist they have never been visited or given any consolation by their loved ones in the hereafter suddenly find themselves feeling moments of joy in the middle of their darkest sorrow, or wake up with the courage to face another day after going to bed the night before wishing they would just die in their sleep, or find the ability to help another in crisis even though their heart is so embittered by anger and hopelessness. What changed then? They are the same people they were the day before, yet suddenly they find themselves coping again, caring again, and they begin the slow process of understanding the tragedy they thought for sure would kill them. The gifts of consolation, given to us and planted in our hearts despite our inability to hear them or see them, are perhaps the greatest gifts of all—given freely by our loved ones whether we consciously recognize them or not. Our ability to continue one more day, walk one step more, and see beauty in life after all the tragedy we suffer is evidence to the fact that the gifts we thought we didn't receive have actually never stopped coming.

THE GIFTS WE ARE MEANT TO SHARE

The gift of consolation is a commodity that is not confined only to the hereafter. We also have the ability to bring the gift of consolation to others who may be just experiencing the first black moments of their grief. The souls have been adamant about not having their messages of hope fall into only a few ears and hearts just because they happen to have been directed to their loved ones still on the earth. They want us to take the message of their wisdom and peace to wherever it might be needed. That is our part of the gift we must share.

Bereaved parents make up the greatest percentage of people coming to me for a session. It is easy to understand why—the souls have told me that without question, choosing the path of bereaved parent in the journey of our life on earth is the hardest decision we will ever have made for ourselves, and the loss of a child eventually affects every aspect of life. There are no other people so conspicuous in their bereavement. Parents who have lost a child will be identified by their loss with friends, family, and associates for the rest of their lives. There is a second wave to the tragedy of having lost a child, which takes the form of guilt, shame, and standing apart from the rest of the world because the most unnatural of losses has befallen them. It is a terribly cruel circumstance in the life of any bereaved parent, but it is the one circumstance on the earth that the Infinite Light considers truly heroic. The souls have told me that great blessings and indescribable joy await bereaved parents at the time of their own passing. The problem is, that will be then, and this is now.

What I have found after working with so many bereaved parents over the years is that although they have been hit the hardest by loss, their capacity to give hope and consolation to another is the most generous. It is also a fact that has not gone unnoticed by their children and the Infinite Light. In our grief support programs, we thought hard about how to help these parents to help each other, and came up with the idea of having a special group program where bereaved parents can hear the communication with their children, and also be in the company of other parents to understand that they are not alone, and that the loss of a child is a life lesson for both the parent and the child—not a punishment by some perverse God. These parent-only groups have had a by-product we hadn't even counted on; these parents at the group would introduce themselves and make friends with other parents who know, understand, and care about what they are going through. It is probably the best illustration I have seen in sharing the gifts of hope we receive from our loved ones in the hereafter.

Our only true gift on this earth is having shared our life with another for even a short time. During times when we can only look at our loss in terms of what we have lost, the real gift comes in knowing that another soul has chosen us to spend its short time with, and the reward is the time we had. If we look at the loss as a tragedy, we will never understand what a gift we received. The soul of a loved one is so much more than the physical presence it took up on the earth. To curse the passing of our loved one is to not understand that our loved one is a complete and total being, on a separate journey from our own, no matter how many times the roads intertwine, and no matter when they separate. We have to look at each other as souls on a course and not physical bodies that are faulted and frail; our souls are invincible and they go on. Our gift is having spent any time at all with another soul that we love. Something given to us even for a second gives us a lifetime of memories, and although I hate clichés, the souls indeed have agreed that it is better to have loved and lost than never to have loved. Imagine never having been touched by the soul of your loved one on the earth—it is an empty experience, and that is real death. Our potential to love, to hurt, to recover, and to eventually learn shields us from true death. At a time when we feel so much has been taken from us, it is the one true gift the souls can give us—a gift of peace.

9.

THE WISDOM

of the

GARDEN–

LEARNING *by*

EXAMPLE

One day in the winter of 1995, we received in the office a letter almost completely covered in stamps from a foreign country. Although it is not unusual for us to receive mail from every corner of the world, this particular letter stood out from among the rest because of the brightly colored images of the Netherlands rendered on the stamps. I picked it up and observed it carefully, turning it from front to back several times to read all the stamps. On the face of the envelope, my name and address was printed very neatly and carefully, but in a curious and artistic handwriting. I had to resist the temptation of opening the letter, because it might contain information about the circumstance of loss by the writer (information I cannot know until after they had attended a session) so

I handed the letter to my assistant, who read it, to make sure there was no information about the writer's loss included.

The letter, written by Mr. Jan De Leur, was an invitation to Holland to speak to a group of bereaved people he knew, who had all read the Dutch translation of *We Don't Die,* and hoped for the opportunity to hear communication from their loved ones who had passed on. It was his hope that due to the special circumstances of the group and their distance from our office, it would be possible to "import" me to Holland, rather than have the entire group come to the United States. He went on to explain in the letter how unique and varied the spiritual beliefs of the Dutch are as a nation, primarily because they are taught to accept differences in people and beliefs, and learn from those differences, rather than to dismiss or scoff at what is not similar to their own beliefs. I must say that this theory is very much in practice in Holland—it is a nation of kindness, openness, and peace.

The thing that most intrigued me about Jan De Leur's letter, however, is that he hinted that one of the circumstances in the group had a historical reference I might find very interesting. Rather than tell me in advance, he wrote, he would like see if this information came through on its own via communication with the hereafter, in order to make the experience more authentic. Because of my intense interest in both American and European history, I have to admit that my curiosity got the better of me, and we set about the process of making a trip to Holland possible.

We had not been able to find time in the schedule to visit Holland until the following May, about three weeks after the tulip season had ended, but I was struck immediately by the beauty and serene feeling that emanates from the country and its people. We were met at the airport by both Jan De Leur and his wife, Raine—a lovely, robust, jovial couple with a rather remarkable command of the English language. I liked them immediately. They were candid and funny, and although they felt that somehow it was an honor for them to have me as their guest, I assured them *I* was more honored to have *them* as my hosts. During the ride from the airport, we talked a bit about my ability, the spiritual beliefs and religions of Holland, and the remarkable sense of peace that comes from the people and country that not fifty years ago was nearly brought to the brink of disaster by Hitler and the Nazi regime. Yet, time seems to have healed many wounds, and the country has not only recovered, it has flourished. We talked about the Dutch's acceptance of differing spiritual beliefs—including belief in mediumship and mysticism—not so much as an evolutionary process, but as a result of having seen tragedy and atrocity on such a large scale during the Second World War. "The eyes tend to look for beautiful things," Jan told me, "after it has seen terrible ones." It came to me in a flash of understanding that both Jan and Raine were old enough to have lived through the war. I apologized to them if my constant questions about that time were uncomfortable for them to answer, but they both smiled, and assured me they knew my interest was genuine.

Since the group was to be held outside the city of Amsterdam, in the town of Amersfoort, our hosts told us that we had time before the group to do a little sightseeing, and they had planned a tour through some of the towns and villages they felt would best represent their country. Some of the towns we visited were Vollendam, a seaside community, where the tradition is to eat an entire cooked herring in one gulp—to hold it up over your mouth and just let it drop. I couldn't do it; the best I could do was watch Jan make a sport of eating the little fish, one after the other. We later went to a restoration village, probably the Dutch equivalent of Colonial Williamsburg, where examples of ancient windmills and wooden shoemaking dot the narrow village streets. At lunchtime, we found ourselves near the town in which Jan lived as a young boy, and thought it might be a good idea to have lunch after visiting the town church, which had many incarnations in its several-hundred-year history—first as a Catholic church, then as a Protestant one after the Reformation, then once again as a Catholic church more than one hundred years ago. The church bore the scars of religious infighting; the original statues of the saints had long since been destroyed during the Reformation, then carvings had been removed from its time as a Protestant church in an effort to restore its Catholic roots. The church was a real testament, Jan told us, to the new wave of understanding and acceptance of spiritual differences in the Netherlands; through religious upheavals throughout its history, and after surviving two world wars, Holland just got tired of fighting.

After visiting the church, we stopped in a café for lunch. This café apparently was famous for their *pankueke*—a type of crepe filled with various meats and cheeses that is a standard dish among the Dutch. Wanting to be a good tourist, I decided to try the dish, and we all ordered one, each with a different variation. As we waited for our lunch to be prepared, Raine pointed across the street to a stone building with a tower, which she explained had once been the Town Hall, where official records were kept during the war. Jan's father worked as a clerk in that building, and part of his job during the Occupation of Holland was to receive the registration cards from all the Jews who lived in the town, in order for Nazi officials to create lists which they would later use for work camp assignments. Jan recalled, as a boy of fourteen, watching the turmoil his father experienced, having to collect the names of his friends and fellow villagers, after hearing rumors that Jews all over Holland were either being deported or sent to work camps, or *worse*. Finding himself back at that moment in time proved to be a little overwhelming for Jan, who became emotional at the recollections, but Raine picked up the story where he left off. "So do you know what he did, this husband of mine?" she continued. "He was just a boy of fourteen, please remember, and he went to the building one day where his father worked for a visit, and then he hid in the tower." She smiled at Jan, who stared at the table in modesty. "He waited until nighttime, and he picked up those cards with the names on them, and then he destroyed them. He set them to fire." Raine looked at Jan again, but this time her gaze was transfixed and her smile had vanished. "They could have killed him, those Nazis; they were furious with him. Instead, they locked him in the building until his father came to get him, and told him, *'Jan De Leur, never come back here.'* This is what Jan did for his town."

I sat in amazement listening to this history of a time when the world had gone mad, and saw before me the living embodiment of what the souls in the hereafter had told me so many times before, *"The true heroes of the earth do good and then disappear."* I found myself honored and humbled to share the same table with them. At about the time Raine finished telling Jan's story, our meals came. The conversation took on a more festive tone as we talked about the differences between the Dutch and the Americans, and the many funny misconceptions we both had about each other as nations and people. Although we were having a wonderful time, I found myself with not much of an appetite and could not finish my lunch. I put my fork down and continued talking, but my eye was drawn to Jan and Raine, and how they set about eating *everything* that was on their plates. When they had finished, there was not one morsel of food to be found on their plates, and I remarked that I felt a little embarrassed, not being able to finish my meal like they had obviously finished theirs. Jan and Raine looked at each other, smiling. "That is because of the war," Raine told me, laughing. "After the war, the Nazis had taken everything from our town—*everything*—and there was no food, no crops—nothing left for us to eat. The only thing there was left were the *tulip* bulbs, and people ate them to stay alive. Eat the bulbs or starve.

Many people knew terrible hunger those days. It was so long ago, but you never forget. Now we eat everything on our plate."

At that moment, I very easily could have died from the shame I felt. I was so ashamed of the fact that I was born to a generation that never felt the terrible, gripping effects of a major war fought in our own back-yard, and the wastefulness we create every day because we have so much. Such powerful lessons come in the most unusual ways. We have to value what we are so fortunate to have been given by sheer circumstance, and to thank the Infinite Light every day for the little things we take so much for granted. Out of my respect for Jan and Raine De Leur, and their courage in rising to the experiences in their life plan, I ate every-thing on my plate that afternoon.

I am very fortunate in my work that I can experience, from a soci-ological standpoint, the differences in people and cultures with regard to loss. Not just loss, but the grieving process, and how society views the bereaved. In Asian culture, it is considered shameful to cry in public, in front of strangers. I recently had a young married couple fly from Japan to the United States with the wife's mother for a session. As my assis-tant brought them up and into the room, I noticed that each of them carried a magazine. It struck me as funny, and I thought to myself, "I guess they want something to pass the time if the session gets boring." They were extremely polite—they smiled, sat with their magazines in their laps, and waited to for me to begin. Within a few seconds, their son, who told me his name was Juki, burst through from the hereafter, hav-ing drowned in a wading pool eleven months ago. When I told them that their son had entered the room and announced himself by name, I saw the familiar, but always heart-wrenching crumpling of the young mother's face into sobs at hearing her only son's name aloud. She im-mediately put her head down, picked up her magazine, and hid her face from me, as did her husband and mother with their magazines. I was touched by their attempt at protocol, even in the face of their terrible pain. I leaned forward, took the magazine from her hands. "You are among your family, your son, and me, your *friend*," I told them. "Cry as much as you need to."

I found very little to worry about with regard to protocol as we assembled for the group session that evening in Holland, because Europeans seem to have a more open-minded attitude about the mysticism of the souls and life hereafter. Rather than undoing the damage and fear of so many in the United States who are skeptical of anything they can't immediately understand, tonight's group would be rather like preaching to the choir—they already understood that communication with the world hereafter is possible, and it is only a matter of what the souls have to say. I also looked forward to the group session that evening, because the souls, untethered by having to *prove* that they exist and are able to communicate, can actually spend their time *communicating* what they came to say, without their loved one's fear, disbelief, or skepticism getting in the way. No matter what the culture, however, two things are always constant—*everyone* suffers after the passing of a loved one, and *all* our loved ones, no matter where they came from on earth, want to reach out to us to help ease that suffering.

The group that evening had the extra bonus of the souls showing me, through different signs, the nationality of some of the attendees. In one session, the father of a gentleman who sat before me showed me the colors of the German flag; in another, the deceased parents of a young man in the group showed me the image of Hans Christian Andersen, an indication to me that their son was from Denmark. When I concluded the session with their son, my eye was immediately drawn to the soul of another young man who entered the room and stood behind a couple seated near me.

"A young man has entered the room, and states he is your son."

"Yes," the couple answered.

Their son went on to identify himself as Ronny, and told me that he had passed on from a progressive illness. During their session, Ronny addressed their concerns that his time on earth was cut short, but he assured them that although it was brief, his was a fulfilling adventure on the earth, and that his parents should consider his life in the hereafter as a continuation, not a termination, of his life on earth. He called out to siblings and family and asked that his family continue praying for him, as he did for them. The next thing I saw was the image of Anne Frank, whose diary during the German occupation of Holland chronicled the life of a Jewish family in hiding during the Holocaust, and drew worldwide attention after her death in 1945. I took the image as another symbol that the couple were Dutch.

"Your son is showing me Anne Frank, so I guess he wants to tell me that you are Dutch."

"Well, yes," they told me, hesitating.

I continued on, but noticed that the same image had appeared again.

"He's showing me the image of Anne Frank again . . . they're telling me that's my clue for the name Anna passed on."

"Yes," they stated again.

The image remained. I thought to this new soul, *Yes, I know you are Anna*, and waited for some other indication that would explain the relationship of Anna to this couple. When I focused more carefully on the image I was being shown, I realized that this was not a symbol of a name or a country—it *was* Anne Frank.

"She tells me, '*This is Anna Frank.*'"

"Yes," they answered.

I looked carefully at the soul before me. It was Anne Frank, the young woman that came to symbolize the power of courage and hope during one of the world's darkest hours. She stood there, serene and smiling, like the images of her I had seen so many times. I thought to myself that this had to be about the most bizarre of coincidences, or my mind had finally snapped and I was seeing things. I focused more carefully on this soul, to listen to what she had come to say.

"She tells me she knows you," I said to the gentleman.

"Why, yes," he responded, smiling.

I found her appearance to be a monumental honor, and I listened carefully to her words. She spoke of being related to the couple in front of me, and rather than focus on the manner of her passing, talked instead about the happy reunion of souls lost during the war. Her mother then appeared next to her, and Anna continued to speak about the disharmony that once existed on the earth between her and her mother. Once they were encamped together at Auschwitz, faced with the grim reality about surviving, mother and daughter came to know and understand each other for the first time in a long time. Their relationship continued until the day Anna was moved to the Bergen-Belsen work camp, where she died of typhus in the spring of the following year.

One of the things she talked about in the session was her immense pride at having accomplished what she had set out to do on the earth— to continue living even after her death. She admitted that not even she could have conceived how famous her "little diary" would become, but she was proud that the words helped teach future generations about the fear, hatred, and evil that reigned during the time of the Holocaust. Before she, her mother, and the couple's son, Ronny ended the session, she repeated the words from her diary that have come to symbolize the very meaning of true spiritual growth on earth: *"I still believe, in spite of everything, that people are truly good at heart."*

After the session, I was invited to the home of the couple I had done this session for, who introduced themselves and Edward and Gabrielle Frank. Edward and Otto Frank, Anna's father, were cousins, and their lives were spared because good fortune had taken them to Indonesia, Gabrielle's homeland, during the Second World War. It wasn't until the war ended years later that the cousins met when Otto emigrated to Switzerland, after realizing the terrible toll the Holocaust took on his family.

I will probably never forget my trip to Holland that year. I learned so much from the wisdom of both the wonderful souls in the hereafter, and the incredible stories of faith I heard from people who have flourished despite crippling challenges to their hope and sense of justice. Yet, they prove by their very existence that faith, no matter how badly it is shaken, can never be destroyed, and that the example set forth by the souls in the hereafter to love in spite of the terrible things that we endure on the earth bear the promise of Eternal Light and, finally—to a world of peace. You have to listen *within* to find the answers, and they are all there—they are in the wisdom of the souls.

10.

FINDING
FORGIVENESS—
in OTHERS
and in
OURSELVES

I have made it one of my personal goals in this lifetime to try to understand a simple fact of life on earth: nothing ever goes the way we think it will. A "sure thing" will vaporize before our very eyes, and a tiny, remote concern will blossom into a hard new reality for us to deal with. I wonder if we intentionally mislead ourselves into thinking that if we can wish something into reality, it will actually happen for us. If that were the truth, no one on earth would ever suffer the loss of a loved one, or experience failure, or find disappointment. Things happen on the earth because they are a reality we must learn from, and there are very specific cards that are dealt to us to keep the right game in play. We must learn from the specific challenges we are given by the Infinite Light, and everything and everyone has a specific meaning and purpose. This is no game of chance, however; the rules have been cast in stone. Yet no matter what we think, there is a method to the madness of life on earth.

I caution people in some of the sessions I do that our loved one's perspective only changes in the hereafter insofar as their spiritual understanding of how the earth worked. They know more now, and understand the world they can now see in its entirety. While they know more now, they don't know *everything*; their thought process changes, but not enough to alter their personality. Life is better for them now, but they are who they are. Sometimes people have an unrealistic expectation of what they think will happen during a session, when their loved one is free to speak as they never could on the earth. Some things do change—the souls find peace and understanding, and it changes the way they thought about a lot of things when they were on the earth. They also understand now from other points of view, which gives them greater insight into our struggles, and their own when they were on the earth. But their personalities don't change so much that they become different people, and their new knowledge can never change the facts of the life they lived on the earth. Being the people they are is part of their spiritual journey even in the hereafter, and through the sessions, they can help us gain some insight into what made them the people they were on the earth.

There was a woman who came to see me that I will call Nancy. She came to see me after the loss of a gentleman that was the love of her life. Nancy was married, and so was the gentleman, but not to each other, and to complicate matters further, both couples were the best of friends. Their relationship spanned many years and continually deepened, but this gentleman would not dishonor his wife by divorcing her and shaming her in a community where they were very prominent. So Nancy and this man continued their relationship, but both maintained the appearance of two happily married people. The gentleman was diagnosed with cancer about the same time his wife was beginning to surmise there had been an ongoing affair between her husband and Nancy. As his health declined, Nancy's opportunities to see him also lessened. At the time of his death, Nancy was devastated that because of their infidelity she was deprived of her opportunity to see him in his final hours and say good-bye to him. In the end, she had nothing left of him but a few trinkets, some fond memories, and continued rancor from his widow. She could not confide in anyone about her pain in losing someone she loved so deeply, and therefore got no sympathy from people who could not know the extent of her pain. Hiding her feelings caused such desperation that she needed the opportunity to hear from him how things would have been different for them if only it were a different world.

The session was interesting to say the very least. The souls are usually not inclined to air dirty laundry during a session, but it seemed necessary for this soul to help me understand the story so that I would not misinterpret his messages, or tell Nancy what I thought he meant. This soul seized the opportunity to set the record straight in a candid and honest way. He regretted not having the opportunity to say good-bye to Nancy at those last moments of his life on earth, but told her that if he had it all to do again, his *wife* would be at his bedside at the end again. Being a man of some principle on the earth, he felt that although his was a loveless marriage and he loved Nancy, his wife deserved to keep her honor and dignity, since she was not to blame for the affair. He also stated that his sense of decency compelled him to keep his wife free of emotional injury by not upsetting her life just because he is no longer around to have to deal with the fallout. He asked her to forgive him for his feelings, wishing he felt differently, but knowing she deserved to hear the truth.

Nancy was stunned. So was I. We talked about her session afterward, and she told me she fully expected him to tell her that it was Nancy all along that he wished to be with those final hours, and damn the fates that separated them in that difficult time. She thought the session would be hearts and flowers. She expected sweet sentiments from a kind lover. But the truth is the truth, and the souls will not disrespect us by simply telling us what we want to hear. This gentleman really stuck to his guns, for good or for bad, hoping she would forgive him for his honest and true feelings. I expected her to be hurt or angry by the statements he made, but she was remarkably philosophical about it. "If he told me anything else," she said, "it wouldn't be *him*. That's who he was, and that's why I loved him."

One of the hardest challenges on the earth is to find a reason to forgive. Yes, it is important to find forgiveness when people have hurt us, but in this instance the souls are not speaking about accepting and understanding the things that happen to us at the hands of another on the earth. But it is as important a life lesson to forgive who people *are* as it is to forgive what they *do*. As the souls have stated many times, the Infinite Light has cast each of us in a role we will play in our lifetime. We will find ourselves in circumstances, both enriching and unpleasant, that are designed to help us accomplish what we are here to learn. But some circumstances may come in the form of others, who are also on their own spiritual journey here. If it is in our plan to suffer the humiliation of loving someone who belongs to another, there will be someone set on the earth whose plan will include betrayal by loving someone when he belongs to another. If we are to leave the earth from the circumstance of murder, there has to be someone whose life plan will go so far off course here that it will include the taking of another life. The souls have told me many times that the wild card in this game we call the earth is *free will*, but I am beginning to think that perhaps our free will is not as free as we thought. If we were actors in a play, we could use our free will to stop speaking our lines, but our free will cannot stop the play. It goes a long way in explaining why things happen to us that seem so random and senseless. If not for the circumstance, we could not grow spiritually. So, in the larger picture of life on the earth, we have to forgive circumstances in people's lifetimes which they may not have any real control over; it is as important in their journey and the lessons they need to learn as it to ours. Forgiveness becomes the mantle for understanding.

I do not want anyone to think for one second that forgiveness is like a giant eraser of the terrible things we do to each other in our struggles on the earth. No matter how much we are forgiven, we are still accountable for everything we do if it is not done in love. There are so many people who have had loved ones pass violently at the hands of another, and sit aghast in the sessions hearing their loved ones asking them to forgive rather than to blame. It is a bitter pill to take when your heart is broken, but our loved ones are not asking us to forget about the past and run blithely through the rest of our lives. They are asking us to *understand* that the circumstance is a part of the spiritual education for both the souls there and us here. It's like the old expression, You can forgive, but you don't have to forget. Forgiveness, however, is a real waterline in the measure of our soul's progress here. We need only to ask two questions if we want to know how we are accomplishing our education here—how much have we shown love, and how much have we shown forgiveness?

I am too human for my own good, and sometimes even I need the souls to remind me about the vital importance of forgiveness. It is not uncommon for me to meet a wonderful, decent family which is loving and kind, only to find during the session what kind of horror and tragedy they have endured in the course of their lifetimes on the earth. Some have lost loved ones to violent crime, terminal illness, and suicide—circumstances where it seemed their loved ones were literally ripped from the earth against their will and for no apparent reason. Even though their loved ones in the hereafter try to help all of us understand that it was necessary to go through such a hard circumstance on the earth to gain such reward in the hereafter, my emotional side wants to get up and scream, "But how does that compensate their families for the pain they endure while they are still here?" What makes it all the more maddening is the dignity and grace these families show despite the tragedies that should have sent them headfirst into bitterness and hatred. Then, since the souls can read my heart, I will be told to stop, and to look at them, to *look* at the dignity and the grace they have. These fine people have learned something through their tragedy that I still struggle with—we must swim in the found peace of understanding or be swallowed up by the tide of pain. So we continue. We struggle to forgive those who wrong us, and we struggle to forgive ourselves. We may fall now and then, but we get up and continue. It takes time to learn forgiveness, but it is our greatest challenge. The Infinite Light is patient and knows this is not a contest. Each of us comes to the field of understanding in our own time.

In a perfect world, each of the sessions I do would bring messages of comfort, answer lingering questions, and set us to complete understanding about our world and the world hereafter. I am fortunate that most of the time that does indeed happen—not because of me, but because the souls are able to go to the very heart of us and communicate the words we need so desperately to hear. Sometimes there are surprises in the sessions, and loved ones say things they never would have told another living soul on the earth, like the mother of a famous actress who told her during a session how jealous she was of her daughter's fame. Sometimes the words are hard to hear, but all of them are necessary. It helps to give us insight into the *people* our loved ones were when they were here, so that we can understand them better, and then learn to understand ourselves better.

Very few people on earth have impressed me with the level of honesty and depth of kindness that can be found in abundance in the heart of my friend Judy Silvers. To me and many others who know her, she represents a rare spiritual example of love that is not often seen; she is able to give so much of what she had never learned to receive. I met Judy a few years ago, through a friend of mine who is a psychiatrist. It doesn't take a rocket scientist to figure out that if a doctor friend of yours asks you to see one of their patients, there will be more outstanding issues that need resolution than just the sadness that comes with having lost a loved one. Without knowing any of the facts, I trusted my friend's judgment that communication with Judy's loved ones may hold some answers to help with some of her issues.

Something about Judy intrigued me almost immediately after meeting her. Although an attractive, well-dressed woman entered to shake my hand, I couldn't help but see in my mind the image of a fragile, frightened child. I hate making snap judgments about people, but the feeling was so strong it was almost comical—to me, it was like seeing a little girl dressed up in her mother's hat and high heels. As we spoke, the planes of her face kept dissolving into the little girl I saw in my mind, so I found myself having to focus on her voice as we exchanged the few words that come with meeting someone new. I asked her to sit down, and we began the first of three sessions it would take to tell the story of her long voyage to understanding.

Judy Silvers understands that the strange die of her experiences was cast before she was even born. Her mother, Fae, was also a product of tragedy. As a young girl, Judy's mother had to watch in horror as her own mother burned to death, after their kitchen stove burst into flames. Although she would later become a beautiful woman and marry a prominent businessman, Judy's mother never recovered from the trauma of loss in her young life, and the effects of that terror marred every facet of her adulthood.

Judy can only remember her young life as a series of frightening episodes of anger and resentment from her mother. She can only point to a few, infrequent times when she and the mother she so admired for her beauty and grace shared a happy moment. Her mother was frequently tortured by depression and psychotic behavior, having to be hospitalized several times in the course of Judy's young life. One of Judy's most vivid recollections of fear came as a young girl, when her mother began ranting during a particularly bad spell that the hospital brought her the wrong baby when Judy was born, pointing to the fact that there was not very much physical similarity between them. She marched Judy to a mirror and told her to look. Judy saw the reflection of a gangly, chestnut-haired girl against the lovely silhouette of the elegantly dressed, raven-haired beauty she knew as her mother. "Look at the both of us," she commanded Judy, as they stood in the mirror. "You are *not* my daughter."

Judy's only precious recollections in her life are those of her father, whom she loved, but acknowledges she has some mixed feelings for. He also feared her mother, and he also lived in the shadow of her violently changing moods. But as difficult as her mother was, Judy was better able to reconcile her feelings toward her mother's emotional instability. Her most heartbreaking disappointment was toward her father, who, in order to maintain peace with her mother, often sided with her against Judy. He seemed powerless to stop the physical abuse to her that he knew about, and Judy feared that telling him about the incidents he didn't know about would incur much worse abuse. Their beautiful home had become a dark island of exile for Judy, and she lived as if it were a war zone with no allies. As she grew into her teens, found more friends, and saw how love and friendship filled the homes of others she knew, Judy resolved to leave the fractured world she lived in, in the only way a young lady could leave a prominent household in the 1960s—she married a man she thought she could love. Within two years, Judy found herself with a child and divorced from her alcoholic husband.

Judy's father died a few months after her son was born. Her mother, whose visits were infrequent since she had no interest in Judy's son, had begun to fall deeper into the pit of her mental illness once she was widowed. Judy remembers her terror when her mother would call, blaming Judy for her killing her father by the way she lived her life. It was a crushing blow to Judy, who felt she had nowhere to turn for support in her crisis—she was living alone with her son, with no family and no money. She felt as if she were an open target for victimization by the mother she once idolized. It was not until her mother's suicide attempt, subsequent hospitalization, and the near-drowning of Judy's infant son by her mother that Judy was able to scramble out from under the thumb of her mother's apparent power over her. Judy resolved to be the best and most loving mother she could be to her own child.

Human nature is imponderable; it can never fully be explained. Although Judy feared and despised her mother, she found herself upset and frightened at the prospect that her mother could actually die from the shock treatments she was being given, because her mother's heart was not strong. Judy still remembers vividly watching in terror as her mother was taken, screaming and crying like a frightened child, to her treatment. Judy was surprised at her own feelings, finding herself heartbroken at her mother's pain. After all the fear and torment, this still was her mother. When she eventually recovered and was well enough to leave the hospital, her mother decided to move to Arizona and live with her family. Instead of being relieved that she was no longer under the hostility and resentment of her mother, Judy was crushed. She found herself feeling abandoned, the same way she was abandoned by her father when he died. As Judy matured and eventually married again, she still maintained contact with her mother, who never eased in her rancor toward Judy.

In 1985, Judy's mother had minor surgery to remove cataracts from her eyes. For some reason, she was allowed to drive herself home after the procedure, even though she had been given an anesthetic. Through a torrential rain, she started the car and proceeded through the town en route to her home. Ten minutes into her trip, however, she fell unconscious and collapsed over the steering wheel. A driver coming from the opposite direction saw what happened, stopped his car, and raced over to her in order to pull the still moving car off the road. She died soon after from heart failure. It was the end of a painful chapter in two lives, both Judy's and her mother's, but it marked the beginning of Judy's search for understanding, forgiveness, and peace.

Judy confided in me, many months after the first time I met her, that in the first session she came to, she was not at all concerned about hearing from her parents. Greg, a dear friend of hers, had recently passed on suddenly, and his passing brought an avalanche of feelings that she thought had been buried with her mother. Since her mother's death, Judy had married and divorced a second abusive husband, adopted two additional children, and married again, this time determined to make things work with her third husband. But scars don't heal easily, and Judy found herself still fighting the demons of her memory. Additionally, her friend's passing put into more painful focus yet another tempest of abandonment: the fact that after her divorce from her second husband, she became estranged from her stepdaughter, who blamed Judy for the divorce and stopped speaking to her. Judy began a downward spiral of hopelessness and depression. She became fearful of strangers, felt worthless, and found she could no longer summon the courage to drive a car.

At the encouragement of a co-worker, Judy decided to seek professional help to work through the maze of fear that seemed to be debilitating her life even now. Through her work with the psychiatrist, Judy began to understand that one of the precious few people she came to trust in her lifetime was her friend Greg. After coming to that realization, Judy found herself having recurring dreams of Greg, and she felt somehow he was trying to get a message across to her. She decided that it was of paramount importance to make communication with Greg, and that maybe his new insight from his vantage point in the hereafter could help Judy in her struggle out of hopelessness.

The session started inauspiciously enough, as many of them do—souls appear, fill the room, and then the soul who has the greatest need to communicate begins sending messages. The only thing that seemed to make this session a little more curious is that the souls seemed to reverse the order; the souls who wanted to communicate came forward first, but the ones who gave me the feeling they *needed* to communicate seemed to stay just out of my periphery. A young man stepped forward, showing me a valentine heart, indicating fondness. Judy understood this, and responded yes. It was the man she had come hoping to hear from, whom she grew quite fond of in friendship over the past few years before his passing. Greg was a man she could trust, and they kept a close platonic friendship until his passing. He admitted during the session that he did have a secret crush on her, but told her that he would be there for her throughout her lifetime here, and that they would meet again in the hereafter.

Greg's communication to Judy seemed more brief than I expected it to be; he spoke, and then immediately moved out of focus. There was someone there who needed to communicate, and that soul stepped forward into my focus. It was a soul who told me she was Judy's aunt. Judy

recognized her and listened intently to her words. The soul asked forgiveness of Judy for not having done more to stop the abuse Judy suffered on the earth. She knew it was happening, but found herself
powerless to stop it without incurring the wrath of Judy's mother. As I
communicated her words to Judy, another soul stepped into the aunt's
place. This soul came through and gave me the name "David," then
quickly changed it to "Dave," and told me to add the title "Daddy." I
could see a change in Judy's face—it went from surprise to gladness instantly. There was a sheepishness to his communication, as if he was not
sure how it would be received by Judy. It was her father, who spoke in
heartfelt words about not having any recourse but to follow the plan of
his life here, wishing there were more he could have done to change
Judy's experiences. He told her that even though his hands were tied in
many circumstances when he was on the earth, he knew Judy loved him
in spite of what happened. As the session drew to an end, I could feel
another soul there, but it was vague and misty. The soul gave me the feeling of a motherly presence, but then retreated again into vagueness.
"Perhaps the soul only wanted to make her presence known," I told
Judy, "but she's not ready." Judy looked at me without responding. The
soul came forward again, this time more strongly, accompanied by Judy's
father. She told me she was "Mother." I saw Judy's body become taut,
but her mother continued communicating, and I had no choice but to
listen. Her mother told Judy that she was coming forward, with Judy's
father, to ask for forgiveness. After seeing the review of her life, she told
us, she understood that she made Judy's life enormously difficult because
she could not control herself while she was on the earth. As I spoke,
Judy appeared uncomfortable and disturbed by the communication. I
tried to help her understand by telling her that it takes a lot of courage
for the souls to come forward and admit their wrongdoing while they

were on the earth, and part of her mother's soul growth is to try to make amends with her daughter. Judy was nonplussed by what I told her, and in fact became more taut and drawn. Her mother continued, asking that Judy try to forgive her for the person she was on the earth. "I don't think I can do that," Judy blurted sharply, looking over my head, as if seeing her mother. I was startled by the anger in her words, but I saw that she was embarrassed by her own outburst. The souls seemed to retreat after that, with a few parting salutations from Judy's father, and the session was over.

I bumped into my friend the psychiatrist one day a few months later, and inquired about Judy, wondering if she had found any value in the communication. To my surprise, she told me that Judy was thrilled with the session—that it was wonderful to hear from her friend, and that she was so happy to have her feelings validated by knowing her father truly did love her. Of course there were issues still left unresolved, as I plainly heard from her anger in the session, but she was working on many of them, and the session was a good launch point for her. My friend asked if it were possible for Judy to see me again, since it seemed obvious that there was another shoe that needed to drop. I told her that as long as Judy felt comfortable with hearing things that might make her uncomfortable, it was her decision. She told me they would consider it.

I would not see Judy again until a year had passed. She had been making some strides in her therapy, and thought that if she were able to face more of the past, the souls would communicate more to her about the issues she needed to have resolved. Now that she was *able* to hear more, she *wanted* to hear more. She came to the second session prepared to face her life. The second time she came, Judy brought my friend, the psychiatrist, for moral support. Although I did remember Judy, I was hard pressed to remember the circumstance of her previous session.

There are so many people who come, and so many circumstances I hear, that it is difficult to remember from day to day, let alone year to year. I find it is always better that way, because the souls can start with a clean slate. We started the session, and I waited for the first soul to come through.

Two souls came together at the beginning of the session, and quickly introduced themselves as "Mom" and "Dad." They began talking about Judy's life when they were on the earth, and I soon began disbelieving what I was hearing. It seemed necessary for them to outline the abuse they know they perpetrated—the beatings, the harsh words, the neglect, tying their daughter's hands together, locking her in closets for long periods of time, and a myriad of emotional abuse that they couldn't comprehend the severity of until they had reviewed it once they had entered the hereafter. They were deeply ashamed of themselves, and likened their torture to a terrorist rampage for much of Judy's young life. Judy's mother stepped forward to tell her that she was not in control, mentally ill, and not able to differentiate right from wrong when it came to her daughter. Then she summed up the total of the lifelong struggle she was so powerless to control with regard to Judy—I felt a pause, and her mother said simply, *"You were my daughter, but I hated you."* I saw Judy stare, transfixed at hearing the words from her mother. There was no emotion in her, just the resignation of final understanding.

I thought there would be some emotional outburst when I told Judy, as carefully as I could, the words her mother needed her to know. I expected some kind of reaction from her, when she heard that after all the torture, after all the abuse, after all the fear—the booby prize she was left with was the simple fact Judy both needed and dreaded hearing: Her mother *hated* her. Somehow I'm sure Judy knew all along that her mother couldn't love her and hurt her so much, but hearing the words takes all

the speculation out of it. Again, both her parents asked Judy for forgiveness, not for themselves, but for Judy. Her life was being held back,
they told us, and she would not be able to find any joy on the earth until
she was able to forgive her parents for the people they were on the earth.
They apologized again for all the hurt and anger they caused, but told
her that it would be a decision Judy would have to make. They can only
ask for her forgiveness, but it would be up to her to make a conscious decision not to live in the pain of blame and resentment. It was up to Judy.

We talked briefly after the session about what her parents said, and
how she felt about hearing after all this time that her fears were justified—that her mother did hate her. Because of her mother's mental illness, part of her life on the earth was a struggle not only with her own
fear and hatred of Judy, but also of herself. Judy told me she was relieved
to have her feelings validated, and the information was not a shock to
her: she felt that someone couldn't be that mean to a child without completely hating her. We had decided to go out after the session and have
a bite to eat, just so I could get caught up with my friend and also cel-
ebrate Judy's sort-of breakthrough. Judy seemed fine as we entered the
restaurant, but as the conversation turned more to the mundane chatter
of life ongoing, I noticed Judy's demeanor was changing. She seemed ir-
ritable and a bit sarcastic. In an effort to soothe what I knew was a back
draft of emotion after the session, I asked Judy if it were now possible,
knowing the whole truth about how ill her mom was on the earth, and
how sorry she is now, that she would be able to put her life in perspective and let the past go. "They don't deserve my forgiveness," she shot
back. "Why should I forgive them?" I told her that she needed to forgive them in order to reconcile it in *herself*, and that until she could find
it in herself to forgive them, their apologies would be useless. But I knew
that reconciliation cannot happen until we are ready, no matter how

much we need it. The session, however, had opened up another can of worms that nobody really anticipated. In all diversion of apologies and hopeful words, Judy came to a sudden understanding of herself that evening—she hated her mother *too*.

Happy endings are subjective things. Not everyone who leaves a session skips out into a world of peace and understanding. Sometimes the session is the last stop in their search for answers, and sometimes it is only the first step in a lifetime of trying to find acceptance of things we can no longer change. More than a year later, Judy came to see me again, accompanied by two close friends. This time I did recognize her, but her friend's loved ones passed on dominated the session. Near the end, Judy's parents appeared together. I could tell from the souls that there was reconciliation between them; there seemed to be a real fondness and a sense of understanding. They addressed Judy together in a concerned, but firm tone, *"You are no further along than the last time we communicated to you. We told you last time that we were wrong, and Mother was not in her right mind. We made terrible mistakes, but you have to learn to forgive what happened and move on. It is your choice. You are hanging on to something that you need to let go. It is your choice."* It was the briefest, most direct communication I had heard in a long time, but they were right. Someone can only apologize for something they did to us for so long, until it becomes incumbent upon *us* to either forgive or wallow in self-pity forever. Her parents were making their peace with Judy, each other, and the Infinite Light. Now the responsibility to complete her own journey fell upon Judy's shoulders alone.

I happened to see Judy a little while ago in a social setting. She seemed different to me now—younger, livelier—and it was perhaps the first time I had ever seen her smiling. I asked her how things were going, and she told me that she was really beginning to feel good, for the first time in a long time. She told me that she finally found the courage to tell people that she hated her mother—not *hate*, but hated. She hated what her mother did, and she hated what those terrible things did to her sense of worth. It is the long, slow process of being forgiven. Not forgotten, but forgiven.

Forgiveness is a breakthrough in our life experience here, and a giant leap forward in our education process on the earth. It is a miracle of our humanity to accept what has happened to us, and while we can hate the circumstances it created, we can learn to forgive the people who create the circumstances. It is the point when our loved ones, the Infinite Light, and the universe are proudest of our accomplishment. It is the point when we begin moving spiritually, with a pure heart and a sense of understanding, toward the Light.

11.

THE CHALLENGE— LIVING *to the* PURPOSE *of* OUR LIFE

The past few years have been very good to me. Not so much because good things have happened around me, but more so that good things have happened *within* me. I went on a book tour for *Lessons from the Light* and had the opportunity to speak to the many people who crowded bookstores wanting to hear from their loved ones—and perhaps maybe meet me too, if it was necessary. Believe me, I have no illusions about why people go out of their way to drive to a bookstore, go a seminar hall, or even come to a session; they don't come to see me *per se;* they come to hear from the souls in the hereafter. This is just fine with me, because the souls are a lot more interesting than I can ever be. I am only the instrument by which the souls can communicate directly to their loved ones, and impart wisdom I could never come up with on my own in ten life-times. In the past couple of years I have come to a more comfortable understanding of why it is necessary to accept that this is, in fact, my life—the reason why I am here. I have come to understand that my life is not going to be a perfect life, but it will be the best way for me to grow spiritually and learn from the experiences I will face. I will accept the joy and the struggle in my life, and even expect it. This is my journey here, my *purpose.* I am completing the challenge I was sent here to complete, with all its good and bad, with all its ups and downs, with all its perks and flaws.

It upsets me sometimes that people don't give themselves the credit they deserve for being the people they are on the earth, doing the things that are in their own life plan to do. Worse than that, it bothers me that some people hold what I do to be more important than what they do, simply because there are less people who do what *I* do, than people who do what *they* do. This came up at a reception after a seminar I did in Seattle, Washington. I was answering questions, when a young lady came up to me and asked, "How do you justify charging money for what you do, since it is a gift from God?" I was stunned at the question. "Why is only what *I* do a gift from God?" I asked her, in return. What everyone does on the earth is a gift—from God, the Infinite Light, Allah, Krishna—whatever you want to call the eternal energy that creates our universe. Teachers have the gift of imparting knowledge, doctors have the gift of healing, even people who have no direction in life have the gift of humility. We are all set upon a path so that we can learn from it here, no matter what the job, no matter what the life. This is the challenge, the gauntlet that the hereafter throws down before us—*"Here is your purpose on the earth; use what has been given you to become an instrument of love while you are here."* Each of us has been given a different set of ingredients on the earth to create a masterpiece. No matter which ingredients we have been given here, or in what amount, we are each capable of creating the same perfect masterpiece. It is all contingent upon our willingness to use what we have been given, not covet what we haven't been given. This is our challenge—to use what we have, and be who we are, to create a perfect world.

GROW WHERE YOU ARE PLANTED

Although the vast majority of people come to see me because they have experienced loss, there have been many people who have come to me after having found themselves at a crossroads in their life. Many feel as if they are swimming in circles, and they seem to have lost focus in their search for meaning in their lives. They come to the sessions hoping their loved ones in the hereafter will help fill in some of the gaps, and point them in the correct direction.

I had a very dear friend call me in a state of panic one day. He needed to see me right away for a session because he heard some terrible news and needed direction. His voice was alarming enough for me to invite him over to have a session that day. His hope was that his parents, who had passed on many years before, could help give him insight into his dilemma. The session began, and his parents moved to the point of his dilemma very quickly—he was slated to be demoted at work. This was a proud gentleman who had worked in his field for many years, and had grown accustomed to the lofty position he worked hard to acquire, and the power and prestige it held. Now he found things crashing down around him. When his company was bought by a larger one, he knew there would be some positions lost, but he never dreamed his prominent position would be in jeopardy. His position was being given over to a member of the new company, but he was invited to take a somewhat lower position in a new area of the company.

His parents helped me understand how insulted and ashamed this proud man was. He had given his life to the company, only to be cast aside by a new team of owners and managers. They also told me that he was upset enough to start making irrational decisions, like leaving the company altogether. This was not a young man, his parents told me, and his options were not many. Their advice to him was so simple it could have been easily disregarded by me, but as soon as I heard the words, they rang with profound truth—*Grow where you are planted.*

We will be shaken out of our comfortable circumstances many times throughout our lifetime. Sometimes it will be through loss, or failure, divorce, our own recklessness, or the recklessness of others, but at some point we will have to return to the drawing board and regroup. It can be a frightening prospect to have to start over again, or to trust again, to try again, or to love again, but the souls in the hereafter tell us the end result has not changed—just our way of getting there. Although we may have been cast to a different road, it will still take us in the same direction. No matter where we must go, or what we must experience, it is so important to the souls that we remember that to change is to *progress*, and we cannot achieve our spiritual goals here unless we are in a constant state of progress. To grow where we are planted is to walk the road we find ourselves on.

I think my friend might not have been too happy with the words he heard from his parents that day. I think he was expecting some hard-and-fast answers, but in our struggles here, there are none. His parents' simple advice speaks volume to how we fight so fiercely to judge ourselves by the standard of others. During the session, his parents reminded him that any position is an opportunity to do good, just in a different area. His new, lower position would put him in charge of training a new crop of employees, which his parents saw as a golden opportunity for him. They asked him to imagine what an incredible impact he can make on the lives of inexperienced but hopeful young people to take pride in themselves and in their work. This demotion in our terms is thought of as a promotion by his parents—the opportunity to give the gift of honesty and integrity to the next generation of business people. All that having been said, we are still creatures of the earth's warped view of what is important—I know it will take some time for him to set aside his pride and see the potential for his own soul growth in this change.

It is important to remember that no matter where we find ourselves flung by circumstances of life here, every opportunity we have to live is an opportunity to grow. We just need to find purpose and meaning in the bigger picture—the advancement of our spiritual lessons while we are on the earth. So many of us are unhappy here—we work in jobs we feel are beneath us, we associate with people we dislike or distrust, and we sleepwalk though lives we can find no value in. Our focus becomes twisted by what we think will make us happy—the sparkle of trinkets, winning the insignificant games we play, and the temporary delight of admiration by others. We have so much to learn. Our most noble achievement on the earth will come in the moments *between* our distractions—the opportunity to listen, the opportunity to give, and the opportunity to love, all without expectation of payment. No matter how lofty or low our placement in the order of the earth, all of us have unlimited opportunity to show the Infinite Light that the message has been heard.

Katharine Drexel, who lived at the beginning of the twentieth century, was recently canonized by the Roman Catholic Church because she was able to see past her station on the earth to her *purpose* on the earth. Born an heiress to a wealthy family, she spent her lifetime and her fortune helping underprivileged and forgotten children find love, comfort, and a reason to live. It is one of the finest examples I have seen of what the hereafter tries to teach us about using who we are and what we have to grow spiritually on the earth and impact the spiritual growth of others. What makes her story all the more unusual is that most people must wait until they have hit rock bottom, financially, socially, and spiritually before they are forced to reckon with their own purpose here. In Katharine Drexel's life, she used the opportunity of her wealth to create her purpose on the earth. This is not an invitation for people to drain their finances, leave their comforts, and dedicate their lives to the single purpose of spiritual fulfillment. The souls understand how the world works because they once lived here. Although we may not have the luxury of spending our lifetime here in the search for spiritual fulfillment, we can still remember from time to time that we have a better set of values to live up to.

A BONFIRE OF THE VANITIES

It has been an ancient custom in many parts of the world that those who were blessed with good fortune show gratitude and humility to the gods they felt made it possible. They would take the items indicating the trappings of their wealth, like money, jewels, or favorite items, and burn them to symbolize how good fortune could turn on them in the blink of an eye. Anything that made them feel more important than others and fine things they coveted would be burned in this *bonfire of the vanities* in an effort to, if only temporarily, remind themselves of the pain of losing the things they hold so dear. As it has been for thousands of years, there will be times in our own lives when a bonfire of our own vanities will humble us and remind us why we are actually here.

Nobody ever comes to see me for a session because things are just going too well in their lives here. It usually takes a tragedy for people to recognize the value of what the souls have been trying to help us with since we first began walking on the earth. It must seem ironic to the souls in the hereafter that it isn't until we have lost everything valuable in our lives that we look to them to find it for us again. The souls, however, are much too compassionate to find any amusement in the irony; they are usually too busy seizing the opportunity to help us in our struggles. They understand how valuable it is, not only to our own journey here, but the souls' continuing journey there, to help us pick up the pieces of our lives and find hope again. Sometimes the wait for us to drop our arrogance and admit we need their help is longer than they hoped, but no matter when it comes, they stand at the ready to show us that everything in our lives is a challenge we will learn from.

Loss is not only confined to the bereaved. We will all suffer losses, of varying kinds and in varying degrees, in the course of our lifetime here. Although we never know where our spiritual road will take us, one thing is certain—if we are on the road here, there *will* be a challenge to face. It is the only way we can learn from our experiences here. No matter what way the circumstance of being humbled appears in our lifetime, it is only a way for the Infinite Light to refocus the way we see our journey here, and to set us again to the greater purpose for which we are here. The Infinite Light has a plan for each and every one of us, and although we will mourn our losses, we must also understand that the experiences are part of the plan. The souls promise that the struggles we endure will be worth every second of the pain we feel, because the reward for our accomplishments is an eternity of joy. We never know where our lives will take us, so it is impossible to curse our fate when things change suddenly for what we perceive to be the worst. Only the Infinite Light knows the why and how in any life plan, and if we have some faith that *everything* is a stone that will build the path of our spiritual purpose here, these bonfires of the vanities will become easier for us, and far less destructive in the course of our lives here.

My friend Maria is a lovely girl whose family I got to know very well over the years. She was the first daughter of an Italian family to get married, which meant a huge wedding, meticulously planned and attended by a few hundred people. She married a good-natured, friendly gentleman whom she loved very deeply, and they set about starting a family immediately. Finances are always an issue in the first years of marriage, and for Maria and her husband every month was a feat of great accounting skills to balance the family budget. Maria had to stop working after the birth of her first child, but they still lived happily on an austere budget, knowing that their new child and new home were worth the few frills they found themselves doing without.

Three years later, I bumped into Maria in the supermarket one day. She now had two children, and enjoyed the fuss I made over how beautiful they were. Something seemed different about her, though; she seemed quiet and drawn. I didn't want to pry, but we talked briefly about the responsibility of raising two children and the enormous pressure that comes with being the custodian of young lives. We laughed about it briefly, but she told me that her husband seemed to be losing his focus on what was really important in his life. She felt that the responsibility of a job, two children, and a new house might be too much for him; he worried obsessively about his finances and often mistook her family's concern for intrusiveness. She held out the hope, though, that in time things would straighten themselves out. They never did—they were divorced a year later.

I didn't get to see Maria again until some years had passed. Life had not been easier for her in those years. Her husband became emotionally unstable, and for the safety of her children and herself, they ended their marriage. The decision did not come without a personal cost, because it was humiliating as a Roman Catholic and as an Italian to be a divorced woman, the first ever in her family. She now had to create a life on her own; to care for her children, manage a home, and make ends meet by herself. Eventually, though, she found the courage to continue, and in fact, became stronger as a result of the hard times. It took a few years of struggle, uncertainty, and loneliness that comes with the life of a single parent, but life eventually returned to normal for her—a *different* kind of normal.

Maria changed a lot in those years—she became stronger, more self-assured, and confident. She now had a new love in her life, and they were making plans for a life together. I was so happy to see that although so much heartache, humiliation, and struggle fell into her spiritual path, it was a struggle that had a very valuable and very *visible* purpose. I asked her once about the hard times, and if she could see them as a spiritual lesson. She was quite candid in her answer. She told me to look at her children. She walked through a very tough stretch of road in her life, but understood why it was necessary—life will take us through our struggles, but bring us to the wonderful place we need to be. Looking back is always easier than looking forward, but faith in the plan of the Infinite Light is necessary. I foolishly asked her if, knowing that things would end up the way they did, would she be able to endure those tough times again. Her answer was simple, "To have these two children—in a *heartbeat*."

STAYING TO OUR PURPOSE
ON THE EARTH

We have a rather liberal sick-day policy in our office—if you need one, take one. There are no questions asked, because we already know the answer. Sometimes, it's not so much a sick day as it is a "mental health" day, when someone just needs the time away to decompress. We work in an office where so few people who call or come in are having a good day; usually they are crushed by tragedy and searching desperately for answers. Periodically throughout the year, we seem to have outbreaks of insomnia that affect everyone in our office. People have trouble sleeping after spending the day living on the edge of raw emotion. Just because we hear of circumstances of tragedy every day, it never gets easier to talk to someone in grief about their loss. Everyone, at one time or another, will reach the point of having heard too much. To have a proliferation of other people's pain temporarily color every facet of life for a while is inevitable, and the only cure is to wait for some perspective to kick back in. No matter who you are or what your belief system, listening to the tragedies of others and their struggle to cope gives us all a feeling of powerlessness that even the communication of the souls cannot wipe away. We are human, and a large part of the human condition on the earth is to feel empathy for another. It makes no difference that we understand the messages from our loved ones in the hereafter that they live on in happiness on the other side. No matter how rosy the picture painted by the souls in the hereafter, we are still here, helping to pick up pieces of people who fight valiantly out of the deep pit of their loss. Having their loss hit *us* where we live is a by-product of working with these brave people—the bereaved.

I feel so blessed that the people who work with me in our office are extraordinarily patient, kindhearted, and good-natured. They also have a wicked sense of humor—they *have* to. It is a way for everyone to blow off steam and allow peace to return after hearing so much pain. Being able to laugh in the face of tragedy is a necessity—it helps restore sanity and normality back to life, and helps keep us to our purpose here.

We seem to find the most humor in the foibles of human nature— mostly mine. My staff likes to poke fun at me about some of the funny things that happen to me either in the office or when we are on tour. They especially love hearing the stories about when things go a little awry for me, and find great joy in my reactions as a result. It is all in fun, so I don't mind—I have to admit that some of my reactions can be pretty funny in retrospect. Some of the funniest stories revolve around the fact that I get very nervous when I'm being driven around by someone I don't know, especially some of the bereaved parents I've met. I don't mean to be insensitive, but we have come to the conclusion in our office that some bereaved parents are the world's worst drivers. It is all said in good humor, and not to hurt anyone's feelings, but the amazing part is that most of the bereaved parents will completely agree that they tend to make a lot of people very nervous when they drive.

We were in a particular city with a lovely couple whose names I wouldn't *dare* mention, because they are such wonderful people—just not the greatest drivers. We were on our way back from a group session for bereaved parents that was a very hard evening for all of us because of the painful stories of loss in the group. The couple was kind enough to drive us back to the hotel, which was only a few minutes away.

The husband and wife talked to me about how helpful the communication was to their friends, the other parents who had made up the group. As each of them spoke, they turned to face me in the backseat— even the driver. It was not long before we rolled though our first stop sign, then through a red light, then around a curve a bit too quickly, before nearly sideswiping another car on the road. They continued to talk to me blithely, with only the occasional *"Oops—it's okay"* interrupting their sentences. With each *"Oops,"* I found myself stamping the floor as if there were an imaginary brake pedal, all the while not daring to look at my assistant, who was crumpled into a ball, shaking with laughter. When we got out of the car and said good night to the couple, they peeled away from the curb, nearly hitting a taxi that was parked there. My assistant howled with laughter once we got into the hotel, telling me how pale I looked, and asking if I actually put a hole in the floorboard from stamping the "brake" so much. Once my head stopped rattling, I have to admit I found the whole thing very funny, and how it only served to enforce our silly generality about the driving ability of bereaved parents. Sadly, it had been the only funny thing all evening.

The bereaved parents I know can readily admit to the mishaps they have incurred—everything from driving through garage doors to backing over their own gardens. They also find it funny, but there is actually a rather poignant fact of life that hides behind the hilarity. Once you lose a child, no parent is particularly concerned about their own life anymore. Losing a child is truly the worst thing that can happen to a parent in his or her lifetime, and although there are so many reasons to continue on the earth—other children, loved ones, and friends—many parents will tell me with sobering clarity that the prospect of dying, ending the pain, and seeing their children again would not be such a bad thing after all. I am not a parent, and can never understand the depth of tragedy one must endure to welcome death as an alternative to pain, but the souls of so many children in the hereafter have helped me to realize that the empty shells trying so desperately here to refill themselves after loss were actually once life-loving people. Feelings of living a life with no perceived worth is the best-kept secret of parents who have lost children. A secret to all but their children in the hereafter, who truly become guardians of their parents' resolve to continue here, despite the want not to.

It is very frustrating for me, as well as the souls in the hereafter, to see that people will fall off their course here and drift from the purpose of their spiritual journey. It is difficult to stay on course when your heart is broken in loss, but it is exactly then that we need to stay the most vigilantly to our purpose. We need to stay on our path so that the difficult, painful lessons we will experience will not have been wasted here. We have to go on, no matter how hard, and stay to the purpose of our life here.

I have said many times that children are my favorite souls to communicate with from the hereafter because they bring so much energy and light with them during the sessions. They can be remarkably strong of mind and heart, no matter what their physical age on the earth, and they are single-minded of purpose when they are communicating to their parents. They also can get away with saying things to their parents in a session that I wouldn't dare say, for fear of incurring the parents' anger. But the children know what to do and how to do it; they know that sometimes the words cannot be pretty when they have to kick us back to our purpose by opening our eyes a little bit. They must help their parents understand the value of continuing here despite a crushing blow to the family, the parents' sense of failure, and even their distorted sense of values after having lost a child. And the children will do it with tact, humor, love—and even some strong words if they have to.

Evelyn K. lost her seventeen-year-old daughter, Marissa, from a teenage prank gone bad. Two rival teams, each in convertibles, had one person stand up in the backseat and "surf" while the drivers slowly picked up speed through the streets of suburban Atlanta. The goal of the adventure was to see which person could remain standing the longest. When it became Marissa's turn, she stood up and "surfed" so success-fully that the driver in her car picked up some speed and pulled ahead of the other car. Concentrating on keeping her balance, Marissa never saw the low tree branch that approached. The branch struck her head, knocking her from the car, but also under the wheels of the car behind them. She was pronounced dead at the scene.

So much was lost that summer evening—more than Evelyn would realize until much later. Gone not only was her precious daughter, but also the strong friendship with her daughter that Evelyn relied upon more and more. "I grew up differently than Marissa—I came from an affluent family where the only thing women did was make good wives for prominent husbands. Marissa was my sanity barometer," Evelyn told me once after one of the sessions. "She was her own woman, and had a wonderful way of cutting through my 'Poor Me' days and bring me back to reality. She was so strong—not like me. I didn't really realize it until after she was gone—she was my only real *friend*."

Evelyn has had two sessions with me. The first was about seven months after her daughter had passed, and it was a poignant reminder to her mom that Marissa was still following her life and helping her "sanity." In that session, Marissa told her mom how important it was for her to find a job to take her mind off the tragedy, and to start get-ting involved with more friends to fight the loneliness. She told her mother that she had to get "back on track" and that her mother had to fight to not drift through the rest of her life here when there was so much she needed to complete. The session concluded, and Evelyn was full of hope, intending to take her daughter's advice to heart and make changes.

The second session was another matter entirely. It wasn't until two years later that Evelyn returned for another session. Since I insist on anonymity of the people coming for a session and it is forbidden for someone to tell me they have had a session previously, I set about discerning the information brought forth by the female presence that barreled in needing to communicate with her mom. There was none of the soft, encouraging language that so often accompanies a discernment of a daughter in the hereafter to her mother here. This young lady chose her words very carefully and spoke very matter-of-factly about the fact that her mom was pampered and idle, and had way too much time to think about how much she had lost. Her next statement made me hesitate, not knowing whether to say it as I heard it, or to paraphrase it somehow. The determined soul wasted no time in telling me to say it as she intended. "Your daughter says you have to get up off your *ass* and find something meaningful to do with your life," I told her. When the session ended, I could see this woman was not happy. "I don't understand," she glared at me, obviously quite annoyed. "I came to you once before, and the other reading was so good. This was *not* my daughter. She would never say those things." I could see how shaken and indignant she was, but all I could do is to explain to her that I had no control over the messages that came through—I couldn't make her daughter say what she wanted to hear. She gathered up her things and smiled weakly at me. "Thank you for an interesting time," she said as she left.

My staff tells me not to open the letters that come to the office. They tell me over and over. They know how I am, and they know what people write. They will tell me about all the letters, but they don't often read them word for word. Sometimes I get letters from people who call me the spawn of Satan, and sometimes I get letters from people who inadvertently include all the details of their loss when they want to come for a session. Some people think I can tell them where their keys are. I get letters that tell me Jesus hates me and someone's cousin Margaret thinks I'm a carnival huckster. You do your best work sometimes and it is still not enough; people will say what they will say because they don't think I am human, and that their words won't bother me. They do. That is part of my continuing purpose that I must stay to—communicating the souls' messages *no matter what*. And I do it all for that one letter where someone will say in earnest, "You helped me find hope."

I saw the letter from Atlanta there, but it looked more like an invitation by the size of it. It was beautifully embossed and the address was carefully written on the front in a lovely handwriting. My curiosity got the better of me, so I popped the flap open.

In it, the card read:

Dear Mr. Anderson—

   You are a liar. There is a special place in Hell for people like you. I came for a session and it was such nonsense I thought I would laugh. I threw out all your books and wish I never heard your name. Shame on you.

                                                            —Evelyn K.

I put the card down, and my face was flush. I felt just like I did when I was a little boy being yelled at in front of the class by Sister Elizabeth. My feelings were so hurt I thought I was going to cry. I didn't even know who she was. I gave the letter to my assistant, who first chastised me for opening the mail, until she saw the look on my face. She just looked at me and said, "George, you can't help everybody find value in what the souls say. Give her some time."

I happened to be in the office a few days later, helping out with copies and staying *very* far from the incoming mail. My assistant came to me with a letter she opened that morning, and thought it was important for me to read. The letter, again from Evelyn, was an apology for the first letter, which she admitted writing in a bad state. She wrote that it bothered her so much to have been so mean in the first letter, she couldn't rest until she got another one out in order to apologize. To me, it was completely understandable—sometimes people lash out in their grief to make someone hurt as much as they are hurting. I would never want to tell her, but her first letter had its intended effect. Regardless, I read the rest of the letter. She went on to write, "I listened to the tape with my husband, and that really was my Marissa. I was so angry at what she said, I guess it did make me get off my ass to stop crying and start pulling myself back together. She had her own way of shaking me from my funk, and this was her way to help me with some tough love. Thank you, and again I am so sorry to take my anger out on you."

I was so glad Evelyn was able to see past the harsh words and understand where her daughter was coming from. I, in turn, had to see past some harsh words in order to understand also. We never stop learning. I think the souls are making sure of that. We create our challenges and we give ourselves the tools to meet those challenges. We can't cry midway that the game is too hard, and walk away disgusted. The challenges don't get any easier, so it is up to us to get tougher and stick with all our might to the purpose of the challenges we will face. Sometimes we pick up on the challenge, and run to a better place with it, and sometimes we don't. Evelyn was lucky—even in anger, she was determined to fight to return to her road, even if her daughter had to shake things up a bit. Although the process was a little unusual, the result is all that matters.

Another thing has come out of Evelyn's experience in writing to me—she has provided my staff another reason to poke fun at me. They tell me the look on my face when I read her first letter was priceless. It's just fine with me. I don't mind the occasional ribbing by my staff, for the same reason the bereaved parents don't mind the occasional ribbing about their driving—because they know they have our profoundest respect. Not just because they have been able to survive a devastating loss, but because they are still able to find some beauty and even humor in the world after so much pain. It is a blessing to know such courageous people, and a real gift in my spiritual education to work with them. We have a purpose, and our challenge is to stay to that purpose until it blooms into a world of peace and accomplishment for us. The souls promise this, and the souls will help us achieve it.

No matter who we are, no matter what we do, and no matter what reason we are sent to the earth to struggle, each of us has meaning. And whether we realize it or not, each of us has incredible value to the world around us and the Infinite Light. The hereafter asks us to try and find that value—not just in each other, but in ourselves. To love ourselves for who we are, and, even sometimes, who we aren't, is one of the most profound challenges we will face. We grow where we are planted—and use the gifts we have to make that happen. I will never be six feet tall, or highly intelligent, or able to program a VCR, but I have value to the world and to the Infinite Light for what I bring to the earth. So do each of us—we possess those marvelous gifts of who we are and who we can be. Stay away from the people on the earth who act like "spiritual vampires," the ones that tell you that you are worthless unless you are *this* tall, or *this* beautiful, or *this* rich, or *this* smart. Tragedy and loss on the earth can be our biggest enemies, but they are also our greatest teachers if we can learn to accept them as part of the cost of our education here. Failure to accept what we can't understand is a cancer that will destroy everything we have worked so hard to achieve on the earth. We are working to become the best only we can become, but it doesn't come without a struggle. We are all perfect in the eyes of the Infinite Light, and our struggle to come to the hereafter pure of heart and soul will reward us with riches we could never have imagined.

12.

CREATE a GARDEN on the EARTH

What if this were your last day on the earth?

Whom would you call? Where would you go? Whom would you mend fences with, and what would you reconcile? Whom would you tell how much you love them, and whom would you tell how much they meant to you? What would you finally forgive, and what issues would you finally resolve? What memories of the earth would you like to take with you, and what memories of yourself would you like to leave behind? Was your time well spent on the earth? Are you ready to go, or is there work left undone?

In so much of this book, the souls talked about the beauty of their world, and the great reward that awaits each of us if we can only man-

age to conquer our struggles here. But what about the earth? Is life here
so hopeless and disappointing that we have to plot and scheme to *escape*
it? The souls have told me constantly, through my own personal experiences and the experiences of people I have met, that life here is what we
make of it. We have the power to decide whether the earth, with all its
struggles, and with all its flaws, will have moments of joy and beauty that
we can remember fondly, or a succession of spiritual failures and missed
opportunities. Many of the souls who communicate during the sessions
actually look back fondly at the earth—many of them had disappoint-
ments and trials here, but many tell me that there were moments of
happiness and contentment that they also enjoyed. Although the souls
acknowledge there was much work to be done while they were on the
earth, they also recognize now that the power to make this a beautiful
existence was in their hands all the time. We also have the power to create joy amidst the confusion, to create happiness in the mire of disappointment, and to create peace in a world of war. Just like Dorothy in
The Wizard of Oz, the power was with us all the time—the power to bring
the ideal of the perfect world of the hereafter to the world we live in—
to create a garden on the earth.

Each of us here has been given a responsibility to leave behind a remembrance of our time on the earth. We have all of our lives to prepare
for it, and all of our experiences here to use as our tools. In our lifetime,
we will take things from the earth in many forms, and in return we must
leave the world a better place than how we found it. Each of us must create our garden, both as a testament of our time here and as a gift to those
left behind who are still in the process of discovery on the earth. How
we leave our garden is how we have lived it, and each of us will choose
what will live in that garden. We will choose for our garden the same way
we have chosen on the earth—to choose hope or bitterness, to choose
love or hate, to choose spiritual life or spiritual death. We can plant the

seeds of knowledge, love, and hope in our garden, or we can leave it bare, having crushed the seeds under a fierce weight of indifference and apathy. Creating a garden of our hopes, our dreams, our triumphs over disappointment, and our courage in the face of pain will be our crowning achievement on the earth.

A GARDEN OF COMMUNITY

I have met enough people through my work and through my personal experiences to say with complete certainty that no life is without struggle. What I find most fascinating about the struggles people have is that they most often have to face them alone. I wonder what is broken in us that we run for the hills when people we know are facing their darkest struggles. I still remember a time when people thought of cancer as contagious. Because no one understood the disease, anyone struggling with this illness generally did it alone. While a difficult spiritual lesson will be learned by victims of cancer, many around them will fail their own spiritual lessons of compassion and caring. No matter how much this century has moved ahead in medical and scientific breakthroughs, we have certainly not made enough progress as a spiritual people. After all the knowledge we have gained and history we have lived through, we need only look to HIV and AIDS all over the world to see that the spiritual lesson of caring or understanding has yet to be learned by many of us. We believe that victims of this illness are unworthy of our sympathy, or worse yet—dangerous to our own well-being. So we try to justify our refusal to care.

Although I understand that it is no better to point a finger of shame than to do something shameful, I know that overcoming the anger of injustice is just one of the many spiritual lessons I have yet to complete.

But the good news is that I know it is *there*. Many of us will not even acknowledge that we are falling down in our spiritual challenges. I find this most often in the friends and families of the bereaved—especially bereaved parents. I find it cruel that often well-meaning parents stay away from parents who have lost a child, either from fear or from worry that the sight of happy, *alive* children will remind bereaved parents of their own loss. I have news for you—these parents *never*, for one second, forget their loss. I have a friend who lost her daughter two years ago, and she called me up one day around the holidays. I could hear from her voice that she was upset, and after several attempts to find out why, she told me quite sheepishly that she was hurt that no one from her daughter's school bothered to invite them to the holiday pageant her daughter was always a part of. What the school failed to understand was that seeing other children smiling and happy gives bereaved parents a sense of hope, and it brings about happy memories of their own children. They also feel that they still *belong*, and that although they have had to face tragedy, life still goes on in some form of normal for them.

One of the most important gardens we can create to benefit others is a garden of community to let others who are hurting know that they are not alone in their struggle. People are all the same on the earth—they want to *belong*. So many people are afraid they will say or do the wrong thing and make things worse. There is nothing someone can do to make things worse for anyone in tragedy. The worst has already happened, and there is nowhere to go from there but *up*. Just the attempt—whether it is successful or not—to show people you care when they are in tragedy is a gift they will cherish. It costs nothing to say some encouraging words to someone who has lost a loved one, a job, a relationship, or some of their hope. There is power in community. In a garden of community, we can lean on each other and know we will not fall when things become difficult.

A GARDEN OF COMPASSION

Call me a patsy, a rube, or a fool, but I give to every street person and panhandler who asks me. I have had people with me walk away from me in disdain after seeing me say hello to someone who has fallen upon hard times and offering whatever is in my change pocket. I have been told more times than I care to hear that the money will only go to drugs or to drink, as if my few coins hold the power to change the spiritual journey of anyone on the earth. All I know is that it isn't the act of giving a few coins, it is the simple act of compassion from one person to another. It bothers me when I watch people on a city street *ignore* someone asking for help, just because there are so many who ask that it becomes an annoyance in their very busy day. They start mumbling things like "free ride" and "get a job" and "I work for *my* money." We are missing the point. These poor souls aren't asking us to decide the value of their difficult life experience here, and we have no right to comment on the state of anyone else's journey here. They are asking to be recognized for who they are—souls who are walking the earth with us.

I got one of my most valuable lessons in compassion fairly early on in my lifetime. I had gone into New York City to buy a book. I had just quit my steady job at the phone company to work as a medium full-time, and I wasn't sure if I would be able to make enough to pay the rent and the bills. Mediumship is not a guaranteed salary, so pennies had to be watched. My one luxury was a book about the Civil War, which I justified by setting some pin money aside for three weeks, knowing that if I wasn't able to make ends meet as a full-time medium, then at least I could drown my sorrows in the Civil War.

As I left the bookstore, I turned a corner and came upon a woman sitting in filthy clothes next to a shopping cart that probably contained everything she owned on the earth. She looked at me and asked, "Spare some change, sir?" My first thought was to tell her that I didn't have all that much myself, but I stopped to actually *look* at her. Her skin and hair looked like that of an old woman, but she could not have been much older than I was at the time. She held out her hand in an almost automatic gesture and looked away, expecting me to pass her without a word. I wondered to myself what could have happened to a woman this young, to wind up with all her belongings piled up in a heap next to her. I fished through my pocket and gave her everything in it, including the money I had set aside for the bus. I didn't realize that I had given her my bus fare until the money was already in her hand, but I felt foolish to ask for some of the money back. She looked at her hand, and then at me, and simply said, "Thanks," as she turned to her belongings. As I stood there, watching her hide the money, a bright image flashed behind her. It was the soul of an older woman who stood over the younger woman as she moved through her belongings. The soul's face was kind and grateful, and I found myself riveted by her presence. She stretched out her arms as if to embrace the young woman, and said to me, *"This is my baby—my daughter. Thank you for acknowledging her."* As I stood there, the soul of her mother showed me a tortured life—a young woman with emotional problems, losing her single mother, wanting to be a teacher when she grew up, finding herself unable to hold a job, looking for solace in drug use, losing all hope. I was so moved by what I saw; a young woman full of dreams at one time, but too fragile to fight her problems, and now fallen down, unable to get back up. That could have been me, I thought to myself; that could have been my life, but for incredible luck and circumstance. I have been spared that pain in my life lesson. "Here," I said to her, holding out my book. "Maybe you want to read it."

"Thanks," she said simply, taking the book and hiding under a blanket. Maybe she would read it, and maybe she would sell it, but that wasn't for me to decide. Behind her, the soul of her mother said, *"Thank you,"* and I continued my walk.

We have all heard the expression, "There but for the grace of God go I," but we seldom understand it. Any of us could have a difficult and unbearable circumstance on the earth—many do. There is nothing we can do to change the life lesson of another soul, no matter how hard we try. But we can touch another human being here with kindness, either in word or in deed, so that they know *someone* has acknowledged their struggle. It takes so little—it doesn't take a book, or some change; it only takes compassion.

To tend a garden of compassion on the earth is to invest in the greatest gift we have to offer—the gift of humanity on the earth. It costs nothing to care, but the difference it can make in the life of another we may never fully comprehend. Very few people on earth are as lucky as I am to instantly see the benefit of such a small gesture, but we will see it—it will never be forgotten by the Infinite Light.

A GARDEN OF GRATITUDE

Some people will argue with me that there is very little on the earth to be grateful for, if you are suffering through experiences here, through loss, disappointment, or failure. We cannot even come close to understanding how the Infinite Light prizes such struggle and rewards it so lavishly in the hereafter. We cannot know, because it would not be a struggle then. I have learned to thank the very things that have happened to me over the course of my lifetime to make me the man I am, even the seemingly senseless or unnecessary. These things were a gift from the Infinite Light to keep me to the purpose for which I am here—to tell people there *is* a reason to continue, no matter what.

We have reason to be thankful every day of our lives here for the miracles we see in the world around us and for the people who have walked near us on their own journey on the earth. We thank our loved ones, both on the earth and also in the hereafter, who have chosen this time and this place to share even a brief time with us, to touch us with their love and their kindness. We thank the opportunities we have been given, and continue to receive, to learn from others more about life on-going. These opportunities provide the road map to be able to fulfill our purpose on the earth. We not only go through our own journey on the earth, but we have a stake in the journey of others around us. Sometimes we will be called upon to teach, and other times we will be called upon to learn. The greatest of these opportunities, the one we should be most grateful for, is to experience love on the earth, and also to share it with others. This lifetime would be a meaningless, barren experience without the opportunity to have given our love to another—regardless of whether it was a short or long time, whether it was accepted or not, or whether we received love in return. The opportunity to share our love makes us worthy of the gifts of love we will receive when it is our turn to join the souls in their place of love and peace. Nothing is ever wasted on the earth unless we ourselves throw it away. No matter how much love we have invested, it will all be returned to us again and again.

I often think of Mother Theresa, who ministered to the poorest of people in India. She had often been quoted as thanking God for the many opportunities she was given on the earth. She was truly a gifted soul on the earth, for her remarkable ability to see the panorama of her life as an opportunity worthy of thanks—to live as a beggar, to know poverty, to feel hunger, to touch those whom no one would touch, and to teach a generation the true meaning of selflessness. We should be grateful for the opportunity to have seen an incredible vision of spiritual light and growth in the person of Mother Theresa, who taught every day the value of pure love.

Being able to feel gratitude for the opportunities we have been given is a rare, bright spot in the garden of our lifetime on the earth—it means we *understand*. We understand that not everything will have a clear and immediate payoff on the earth, but we will benefit if we can hold out in our hope. To be able to thank the earth for the experience of being able to laugh, to cry, to dream, to suffer, and to find peace is the key to fulfilling our spiritual lessons and to grow into the perfect beings we will soon become.

WALKING IN THE GARDEN OF OUR OWN MAKING

As you walk through the garden of your lifetime here do you like what you see? Has the work you are doing borne fruit, or has neglect left need for some more work? How much longer will we have to toil on the earth before we can rest in a field of peace, harmony, and accomplishment? Maybe it is today.

Live your life every day as if it were a garden, and tend your garden as if today were the last day you will touch it. The Infinite Light, which has given us so much, asks so little in return. We are asked to create a garden for ourselves and others while we are here—from whatever we can find, and whatever we can do. We create the circumstances we will learn from while we are here by cultivating the opportunity to grow as souls of light—in choosing right from wrong, in choosing to grow from the experiences we endure, rather than just survive them, and in choosing hope over despair. We will be called upon many times in our journey here to prove that we have been listening to the souls and the Infinite Light, and then, one fine day, we can put down our tools and continue to a place where there is no pain, no struggle, no heartache, no disappointment, and no fear.

Walk on, knowing the garden of peace is just up ahead; just over a hill of constant torment, past the rocks of hurt and anger, over the brook of constant worry, past the weeds of intolerance and hatred, to a place of such perfect peace that even the ground feels soft and receptive beneath your feet. The fire of true love can be rekindled there by a carpet of heather, and reconciliation with the past can happen in an open field of understanding, lit by a golden sun of forgiveness. Turmoil and anguish disappear under a shady tree. Trouble never lived here and peace will never leave. No one ever grows old, no one ever becomes ill, and no one ever dies. One day, each of us will find our way to that world, and find ourselves walking in the Garden of Souls. Until then, tend your garden—in happiness, in peace, and in hope.

13.

ASK GEORGE ANDERSON—QUESTIONS ABOUT LIFE HEREAFTER

On September 1, 1997, George Anderson Grief Support Programs launched www.georgeanderson.com, a website devoted to bringing information, insight, and a sense of community to bereaved persons all over the world. In hoping to address many issues that concern those who have lost loved ones, georgeanderson.com included a page entitled, "Ask George Anderson," where people could ask questions about life in the hereafter. Within the first month of its debut, "Ask George Anderson" received more than one thousand questions about life, death, and advice about coping with grief. By the first anniversary of the website, there were more than fifty thousand emails, letters, and faxes from people in forty countries who sought advice from the souls and George Anderson.

To date, nearly four hundred thousand people have visited the website to read, learn, and share information about life here and hereafter. The following are some letters where George addresses issues that concern people struggling to find peace.

Dear George:

If a person is dysfunctional in life, is it possible that they are still dysfunctional in the afterlife? Do they have work to do before they can be in a position to give advice?

When we graduate to the hereafter, we learn all about the things that happened to us on the earth and begin to understand them. The soul, free of hurt and hopelessness, becomes perfect again in the hereafter. We never lose our personalities because that is what makes our soul unique, but we do lose the dysfunction that plagues us sometimes in our existence here. Now you know why they call it "Heaven."

You state in your books that in the hereafter, all the spirits have to do is imagine whatever they desire and they will have it, such as cars, mansions, etc. But if they miss us like we do them, don't they ever imagine being with their families again? You stated that they usually don't want to come back, but rather wait for us. I can't believe they don't miss us and hurt as bad as we do here. Or are they numb to emotional pain there?

The souls don't miss us because they are with us all the time. Just because we can't see them does not mean they aren't there. They still consider themselves part of our family, and they are involved in the good and bad times of our lives until we are ready to graduate to the beauty of the hereafter just like they did. The souls also communicate the best they can by sending us feelings of being loved, whether we recognize it as communication or not. They just want us to know that we are loved and we are not forgotten by them. They also know that when we are finished here, we will join them in the hereafter, and it will be as if not a second had passed since we saw them last. The souls have patience because they know how soon it will happen—for us, we must continue our lessons on the earth until we are finished.

I've recently lost someone to suicide who has been contacting me since his death a few weeks ago. I'd like to be able to assist his soul in reaching a higher plane of existence than the one I fear he is currently on.

Don't worry about your friend. He is not on any dark plane; no suicides are. The Infinite Light is compassionate and understanding when it comes to people who have passed by their own hand, and will do whatever the soul needs to recover and learn from this mistake. You are already helping your friend more than you know by praying or thinking about him, which sends spiritual "hugs" to the hereafter. The souls will appear to us, not because they need anything, but just to let us know that they have reached their destination and are trying to help *us* cope. They do this because they care a great deal about us and don't want us to get bogged down in the circumstance of passing, but rather that the transition was made and completed.

I heard you on a radio program recently out of Seattle and you were wonderful. I missed the part where you were talking about the difference between a psychic and a medium, though. I wonder if you would help some of us understand the difference.

Your question is a good one, because there is a big difference between psychics and mediums. A psychic's ability rests in being able to use his or her ability to discern information *about* a person, on the earth or in the hereafter, mostly with regard to the things they can pick up mentally. They can also use their ability to predict future events. A medium uses his or her ability to *hear* the transmission of information from that same loved one in the hereafter, and communicate actual messages from the souls there. I have found that most mediums are terrible psychics and cannot predict the future, because if a soul isn't speaking, there is nothing for the medium to communicate. There has to be that link with the person in the hereafter to make mediumship possible. A lot has been said that anyone can be a medium, but I have to tell you honestly that I don't think it is possible to train yourself to be a medium. I think it is like having blue eyes—you either have them or you don't. But you don't have to be a medium to hear directly from your loved ones—they try all the time to communicate to us and hope we understand their signs as an attempt to let us know they are happy and at peace in the hereafter.

I have absolute faith in the hereafter as this faith makes day to day life livable. I work with the developmentally disabled population on Long Island, New York. The people with whom I have been blessed to care for are profoundly retarded and unable to communicate in any way. I am very attached to these special human beings and have often found myself "talking to their spirits" while dreaming. I wonder if this is possible, for souls to communicate out of the body, while still living in the body. These dreams have given me better insight into the individuals so I am better able to care for them. I often dream of one person in particular. I have always been very connected to the afterlife and have experienced contact in the dream state for many years. I was wondering if this communication could be possible, or are these just dreams?

Your question is a complex one but has an easy answer—yes. Some souls whom I have discerned as "passed on" are actually still on the earth, but incapacitated in one form or another. Very often this will happen with a victim of Alzheimer's disease, because their soul makes the transition back and forth (from here to the hereafter) until the physical body ceases. It is not always the case though, but sometimes souls can free themselves from an incapacitated body to communicate in much the same way as they communicated to you. Consider yourself very fortunate that these souls care enough about you to "bend the rules" a little to communicate to you.

I really am beginning to understand that even though it is torture to endure the loss of a loved one, we have to see things as lessons that we (hopefully) can learn from. This may seem like a dumb question, but have you had any losses that you couldn't deal with or does your ability prevent you from feeling the same grief?

That is not a dumb question at all—in fact, it is probably the one most frequently asked of me. I have had losses in my life that I also struggle with, not because these loved ones have passed on, but because I really miss the physical—seeing them, having fun, and just hugging them

sometimes. I think that all bereaved people grieve the loss of the physical loved one no matter how much they understand that they continue
on in the hereafter.

Because I am human and on my own spiritual journey on the earth,
I go through the same grief process. When my dad passed on, I knew
that eventually he would make his way to me to let me know how he was
getting on in the hereafter. It was a huge comfort to see him happy and
in good health again, but I still miss those times when we were together
on the earth. It is like having loved ones in another state—you can communicate to them over the phone, but nothing is like being together. We
are all in the same boat that way!

*Do souls have to develop communication skills once they enter the hereafter? Specifically,
is it easier to contact a soul who passed on many years ago as opposed to someone who
passed on more recently?*

It does not make a difference how long or short a time someone has been
in the hereafter—they instinctively learn how to communicate back to
us. They want so much to let us know that they are fine, but also they
need to allow us to grieve and move on our own for a while. When we
are ready to hear from them, they will communicate. P.S.—You don't
need me to hear from your loved ones. When the time is right, they will
let you know they are around.

*I was a victim of childhood sexual abuse by a neighbor. It was severe, and went on for
a period of seven years on a regular basis. This person has since died, which is how the*

abuse stopped. I have spent twenty years wondering if he has had to "pay a price" for his actions and the subsequent harm it has done in my life. This may sound strange, but I do believe (sometimes) that my experience has led me in many positive directions. I work in the human services field with developmentally disabled adults and those in recovery from addiction. I never knew my natural father as a child. But when I did find him later as an adult, he told me that he had spent eleven years in prison for child molestation. He is dying now, and has asked me for forgiveness! I don't know if that is up to me. What will happen to him when he dies? As victims of abuse, I think we all hope that justice will be done if not here, then "there."

I'm glad you understand that everything that happens to us on the earth (even terrible things) are experiences that will teach us something we will need to enter the grace and beauty of the hereafter. You have learned to persevere through a horrible experience, which is a very valuable lesson.

Don't worry about those who have done you wrong. Nobody escapes the wrong they have done on the earth. Everyone who has done terrible things to another must reconcile and understand the terrible things they have done, and have to work hard to continue forward to the Light. It is also time for you to forgive. It is the hardest lesson to learn on the earth, but the most valuable. Give yourself time, but allow yourself to heal by forgiving those who most need your forgiveness now. You will be the spiritual champion now.

I had a discernment with you recently and it was incredible. What I found to be the most interesting is that your assistant told me not to ask any questions until the end and that my wife who passed on would know what I needed to hear. She was absolutely right. How do the spirits know what we need to hear?

During the session I tell people not to ask any questions because I don't want any information from the sitter. My job is to listen to your loved ones in the hereafter because, in essence, the session is for them. They are the ones who decide what they want to talk about and I just listen and communicate that information to the sitter. No matter what happens I cannot make your loved ones tell you what you want to hear, but in most cases they are willing to talk about the subjects we need to hear.

The souls in the hereafter also want to prove to us that they have been listening to us when we talk to them. During the discernment I find that they will have answered questions without even having been asked because they know it is on your mind and they want to help. But again, it is their arena and they will communicate the information that they feel they want to talk about.

I try to remind people that their loved ones are cramming a lifetime into an hour or so, so they won't get to everything you wanted to know about, but they will do the best they can to accommodate us so that we can find peace. It is not always what you want to hear, but the information is certainly what your loved ones know you *need* to hear.

I always believed in the hereafter and after reading your books, my faith in it is even stronger. What I would like to know is how can one decipher messages given to them from the other side in dreams? I lost custody of my daughters during my divorce and haven't had contact with them in over three years. I frequently dream of loved ones who have passed on, and they also seem to give me "updates" about my little girls. Could this truly be happening, or is my imagination getting the best of me?

It is very common that the souls in the hereafter want to help us with the bigger issues in life—that is, if they are able to. Some things they cannot change for us and understand that it is part of our learning on the earth to go through bad experiences. But they will try to help us where they can; even to give you "updates" about your children.

The unfortunate part of visitations in dreams is that there is so much our subconscious mind will not let us remember. It is probably for our own good, but the wonderful feeling of having been visited is the thing that stands out most from our dreams. Even though you can't remember what these wonderful souls have told you, your subconscious mind and your heart will remember and the messages will still bring you peace. Enjoy the updates and be sure to thank those very special souls in your life who care enough to help you through a tough time.

I strongly believe in reincarnation and from your books, it sounds like you can spend as much time as you choose before you return in a human form. Is this true? And do you really accumulate knowledge and experience and work toward a greater existence somewhere else? Perhaps to a "place" when you decide you don't "have" to come back. And can you choose who/what you want to be next go around?

You are absolutely right—the decision to come back to the earth is a very long process in the hereafter because the souls continue learning and understanding in a place far less crazy than the earth. Some souls have told me they will never come back because it was just too hard. We do choose our next life on the earth, not so much by what we would like but rather what lessons we can learn from that lifetime.

P.S.: Never forget that our loved ones will always wait for us to return to the hereafter. It is as important for them reunite with us as it is for us.

I have a best friend who "disappeared" two years ago. I do not know if she is dead or alive somewhere. I was wondering if you have ever given a session to someone and at that time they found out that the person had passed on? That would be quite a shock I would imagine. Has it ever happened and how did the person respond?

There are a few people who had loved ones missing that came to me hoping that I could provide some information about them, but I caution them that I hear from the souls in the hereafter, so if I can communicate with them, their loved ones are already there. It has come up in sessions, but usually their families are at least glad the issue is resolved one way or another. It is a hard issue for the family to face, but sometimes knowing is better than not knowing. I also think that some of the people who have come to me about a missing person already suspect that they might have passed on. That is not unusual because statistically, most missing persons have been victims of foul play and have passed on as a result. At the very least, during the session they are happy to clear up the mystery for their families and to let them know that despite what happened, they are all right and at peace in the hereafter.

When a celebrity dies and they didn't know you on earth, can they still hear what you say to them, and know what's in your heart for them? Also, what does it mean when you experience lots of coincidences and synchronicity around someone (celebrity or otherwise) who has recently passed on?

The souls, no matter who they may have been on the earth, hear your kind thoughts about them. During a discernment though, they are less likely to come through because the souls of your loved ones want to communicate, and they do not want to take any time away from them. But they know how much they are thought of and they appreciate it.

In a group discernment once, a gentleman was there who heard from his father, and then a "Grace" came in very briefly to say thank you to him for a job well done. It had a very big impact on him. A few weeks later he wrote to me to tell me that the "Grace" who came through so anonymously in the group was Princess Grace (Kelly) of Monaco. This gentleman turned out to have written a biography on her life, and had always wondered if she was happy with the way he had portrayed her life in the book. It was nice that she took that brief opportunity to respond in a special way. In the hereafter, "stars" get to be "just people" again (which they want), so it is rather special when someone who was notable on the earth comes through in a nonfamily session.

As we begin the 21st century, how does the outlook for open awareness on life after death and grief support look?

If you asked me twenty-five years ago if I thought that this field would still be mocked by the "experts," I would have said yes. I am actually stunned (but glad) that people have dropped the arrogance that made them believe this is "it" and you only go around once, so *grab* what you can. People are beginning to understand that we are here for a purpose and to learn from this existence. We are accountable for what we do on the earth, but we are also loved by a power much greater than our own. I am also glad that the bereaved understand this rather than think that their loved ones are gone forever.

Months ago you helped me with a question that has totally changed my outlook on the passing of unborn children. Now I am dealing with my elderly mom suffering from a progressive illness. I am an only child and to watch her become so frail and having to lose her is making me profoundly sad and afraid. I am married, but an only child and my mom lives downstairs from us. Is it normal to feel grief even before someone passes? When my dad passed 20 years prior, I became ill with pneumonia followed by a chronic illness. I cannot control how my body reacts to sadness and wish I was stronger in that respect. I know you experienced the passing of your dad too. Any suggestions on how to get hold of my strength and faith? A priest friend of mine said I should not feel badly that I am so sensitive—yet I see people get through their grief so well. Your book, Lessons from the Light *has been a great comfort and I thank you. Actually, I guess I am asking if I am alone in feeling this way or do others suffer these emotions and physical stress and how should I cope "through" these?*

It is possible to grieve for someone before they have passed because the person that you knew is not the same anymore. Most people are also grieving for the life they had before a loved one got sick and so many responsibilities are heaped upon them. It is very natural to feel that way, and don't be ashamed of your feelings. You are not alone.

The souls in the hereafter tell me that all the hardship we experience on the earth is for a reason, and we will know the reason only at the time of our passing. You are also helping in the soul growth of someone who has to rely on you for help—often a very hard experience for them too. There is a special blessing from the hereafter to those who care for a sick loved one because it is so difficult. Hang on, though. The benefit to you in the hereafter will far outweigh the pain you go through now.

I have a very dear friend who has HIV. I know one of his greatest fears is pain. Is dying painful? If it is; is there anyway to ease that pain?

Passing on to the hereafter is not painful, but the dying process may be. There is no way around it, but the souls in the hereafter have told me that they do not regret a second's worth of suffering that they endured prior to leaving the earth. Why? Because these souls are blessed in a special way for their suffering, and benefit greatly from the experience once they enter the hereafter. I had a young man who passed from leukemia come through to his parents during a discernment. It was a painful last couple of weeks for him, but he told me that he would go through every second of the pain again to benefit in the hereafter the way he has. The souls also tell me that nothing happens here without a reason, and we are rewarded at the end of our struggle. I hope your friend can focus on this instead of the pain. Good luck to you both, and ask the souls there for help when things get rough.

How can I learn to believe in life after death? I am so stressed, at times I don't know if I can go on. I worry about death. Maybe not death, but dying. I want to believe, but don't know how. I want to seek out someone with the answers, but who? I have read about you and feel you truly have a gift. I don't want a fly-by-night that guesses at what I need. Can you help or recommend anyone?

From my experience in receiving communication from the souls in the hereafter, I have learned that no one can teach you to "believe" in life hereafter. It is not necessary that you believe in a hereafter—it will be there for you when it is your time, whether you believe or not. I know that many people say that if you don't believe in "Heaven" you won't go there, but that is absolutely untrue. Everyone, regardless of their beliefs on the earth, will experience the joy and peace of the hereafter. Many of the souls that now communicate to their families here marvel at how wrong they were about the other side. They are very happy to have been proven wrong. The Infinite Light is a destination, not an option.

Even the souls in the hereafter cannot spoon feed us through our lives by giving us all the answers. They understand now that everything that we suffer through on the earth is a lesson that we must master on the earth so that we can benefit from it in the hereafter. They would never take away our opportunity to learn, much the same as you would never deny a child an education, even though you know that school will be tough.

You don't need a medium—you need someone on this plane to talk to! My best advice to you would be not to look beyond right now, but to look *within*. The strength to face the lessons of the earth is within all of us, and it just needs to be focused. Counseling is always a great way to focus from within. Once you get a handle on this world, then worry about the next.

I have read in your articles that we choose our destiny and how long we stay on the earth. My religious studies say that everything is in the hand of God— even a leaf falling from a tree. Can you tell me how can a child who was the happiest girl anyone around us had ever seen would want to die ? On the other hand, how can God be so cruel to cause her death? Lastly, have you ever contacted anyone who wanted to come back to this world but can't?

Suffering the loss of a child will be the most difficult challenge asked of you on the earth. It is not an issue of a child wanting to die, or a cruel God causing her death. It is just a matter of completion. Some of us will need eighty or ninety years to complete the life plan we have set for ourselves, and others are more spiritually advanced, completing their lessons sooner. Sometimes a life plan includes a very brief time on the earth, and another life plan will include suffering the loss of a child. Our plans are intertwined.

We will never understand how misunderstood the concept of "death" is until we experience it ourselves. The souls have told me repeatedly that death is only the gateway to the reward we will all earn in a magnificent existence. Some just complete the journey faster than others.

Each of us is on a road here, and we have things to accomplish. Some lessons are short and some are very long. The souls in the hereafter have helped me to understand that no matter what your age on the earth, when you are finished with your work here, you get to return to the magnificence of the hereafter. We cannot understand this because we think dying is losing something. It is quite the opposite—dying here (after our work is done) is gaining everything. There is a reason for everything, good and bad that happens here, but we benefit from everything we learn here when we ourselves return to the hereafter. This is something the souls there promise us.

I wanted to know how people in the hereafter are told that someone is meeting with you and how they know to communicate with you. I had a session with you the other day and found it completely amazing. There were about twelve relatives of mine there. I just don't get how they know?

Thank you for the compliment, but I am only the instrument. The souls in the hereafter tell me that they listen to every word we say to them, and they also draw close to us when they are needed. They seem to know that we have a need to communicate to them, and knowing that

I can translate their words and feelings, they use the opportunity when we are together to communicate through me to you. Just the same way you knew to set aside time for the session, your loved ones also know to set aside the time so that they can tell you what they want to tell you. I often tell people that you can communicate to them anytime you want to by just thinking of them or speaking to them, and the sessions with me are their opportunity to "answer." If the souls there have a need to communicate during the session, they will, but if there is someone who has more of a need, that person will step aside so that the one with the most need can communicate. But they all are there—it is as important to them to communicate with us as it is for us to hear from them. They are just as excited to be able to tell us that they are well and at peace in the hereafter, so they look forward to that opportunity to tell you through me. It just goes to show you that no matter where we go, here or hereafter, we still want to "check in" with the folks at home and tell them we're fine!

For as long as I can remember, I have never appreciated being alive. It seems from the time I was very small that I looked forward to the day I would die. I guess I'm worried because I believe I should consider my time here and my very life as a gift. When my time comes, how will I face God knowing that I never appreciated my time here? How can I learn to see my life as a gift? This lack of appreciation feels like my greatest failure.

Life on this plane is not so much a gift as it is a test of faith and endurance. There are some people who do feel that it is wonderful here, but if you asked most people for an honest answer, they would have to say otherwise.

Life is hard for a reason. We have to go through these struggles so that we will benefit from our hard lessons when we pass into the hereafter. Life hereafter is a gift, but it is a gift that was bought by us with a lot of work. The souls in the hereafter have told me emphatically that there is a reason why everything happens in our lifetime here—that is the only comfort they have for the living. They promise that when we reach the other side, we will be glad we went through it all, because the joy and happiness we experience there makes this existence worth the trouble. Ask your loved ones there for help, they are already helping you more than you know, and they listen to every word we tell them.

Hang on the best you can—believe me, the end result is worth it.

I am a twenty-two-year-old black female, recently diagnosed with Non-Hodgkin's B-Cell Lymphoma, third stage. My oncologist and primary care doctor have given me a prognosis of approximately 11 months to live. Over the past few months the thought of death has been on my mind all the time. I have publicly kept a good attitude but inside I am SCARED. I have always tried to be a good person but in the past I have done some things I'm not proud of. I am afraid that I will not progress into the next stage of life because I am having a difficult time forgiving myself. I recently read your book and I figured that I would drop you a line to see if maybe you can help me. If so, please reply—I would appreciate it very much.

The only thing frightening about passing is being told you will pass. The consolation is that EVERYBODY is going to pass on into the love and peace of the hereafter—some sooner and some later. Don't be afraid.

The souls in the hereafter have told me that passing into the hereafter is as easy as walking from one room to another. When we are ready to cross over, we are helped through the transition by people who know and love us, who are already there. They will help you and answer all of your questions.

I can tell you that from my personal experience in communicating with the souls in the hereafter, the Infinite Light is more understanding, forgiving, and compassionate than anything you could imagine. We are not punished for the things we are truly sorry for—we come to terms with those things and work them out in the hereafter. *Nothing* is beyond the understanding and forgiveness of the Infinite Light. When you cross over to the hereafter, you will come to the full understanding of everything in your life that was a spiritual lesson to bear, and you benefit from all the things you had to go through on the earth. Nobody that has come to me in a discernment has ever expressed anything but joy about being in the hereafter—they tell me it is a wonderful existence where everything we were deprived of in this lifetime is fulfilled.

Keep in touch with me from time to time, or if you start to lose your nerve if things get rough. You are not alone, and your loved ones in the hereafter will help you any way they can—just ask them.

Do our loved ones who have passed on know our every thought? I lost someone very close to me three years ago, and at the time we had many conflicts in interest and I felt a lot of resentment towards this person at the time. Since her passing I have not been able to forgive myself for having negative thoughts and am wondering if she knows that I love her and if she can ever forgive me? My daily thoughts about these questions hurt me very badly. Can you tell me what I can do to make this person know that I am sorry?

The souls in the hereafter have told me that upon entering there, they get to understand the reason behind everything that happened on the earth, including relationships and how people really feel.

The souls don't want us to dwell on a handful of arguments or some bad feelings over the course of a lifetime. Just like the old adage, a few bad apples will not spoil the whole bunch. Of course your loved ones know how much you care! They know that things are said or done that we don't really mean, and they forgive us and want so much for us to forgive ourselves. Love is the only bond that can never be broken, here or hereafter.

The souls in the hereafter always ask during a reading that we pray for them or even talk to them out loud. They still consider themselves part of our family and are always listening, and they appreciate being thought of. Tell her how much you love her—she loves you too, and waits for you in the hereafter.

Have you ever had a private session with an individual and were not able to contact the person they wished to receive a message from. In private discernments are you always able to receive messages from the person(s) that individual wishes to contact?

In the twenty-seven years I have been working professionally as a medium, there has *never* been an occasion that no one has come through during a session. Why? Because as much as you need to hear from your loved ones in the hereafter, they also have a need to communicate to you that they are happy in the hereafter and that they have not left us. The sessions are as much for them as they are for us.

I love animals and have had many pets. Will I be reunited with them when I pass on? I have had to put one dog to sleep at two years old, another passed on at six years old while we were away, and another passed on at fifteen years old while at the veterinarian's office.

It is very painful to lose them and I will always miss them, but the worst part is not knowing if they understand how dearly they are loved. Do they know that they were not abandoned and I wish with all my heart that I could have been with them when they passed on?

Contrary to the beliefs of some religious organizations, all our beloved pets are in the hereafter. I have been told by the souls there that anything we love or loves us passes on to the hereafter and becomes part of the love and peace of the Infinite Light.

Although pets do not speak, they can communicate their feelings during a session and also let their loved ones know that they are in the hereafter. Very often pets are called to duty in the hereafter to help cross someone over, or to help convey a feeling of peace and well-being to someone who has had a difficult transition, as in suicides.

I have also been told by the hereafter that pets are the closest thing to the Infinite Light on earth since they love without condition and forgive without question. Could you think of a finer friend?

Your pets know how much they mean to you, and they are still with you. Shortly before my father passed on in April, he told me that our family cat, Booboo (who passed on fifteen years ago), came to sit with him. It made the world of difference in helping him face his passing to the hereafter. As with my father and everyone else who loved a pet on the earth, your pets will be waiting for a happy reunion when you cross over.

I lost my father, my older brother, and my younger brother, and his only child. It has been determined that our family has a rare genetic disorder leading to cancer and the immense suffering it causes prior to passing.

My question is this— we all must die, I realize, but why do some suffer so much more than others? The karma explanation can be hurtful to families like mine who have witnessed such enormous tragedy, time and again. The notion that those we love and watch suffer somehow "deserve it" or are paying for past sins adds greater pain to an already unbearable struggle. Because my young sister and my mother are battling cancer right now, and the rest of us and our children are at risk at all times, it would help to know what those on the other side say about suffering here. Why are some singled out for so much tragedy?

It is very hard to watch the people we love suffer, and we always do one of two things—blame God (or the Infinite Light) for "smiting" us, or blame ourselves for something we must have done to deserve this, as if anything we could ever do on the earth could punish us more than watching loved ones suffer. I will tell you this—the "karma" explanation is very much misunderstood.

The souls in the hereafter have told me that every experience on the earth (good and bad) is a lesson that we benefit from when we pass into the hereafter. In a way we do choose our fate or life journey (not to suffer horribly, but to learn from suffering) but we are *not* "paying" for past sins—that part of it is not true.

The best way I can illustrate this to you is through one soul's experience in the hereafter. The parents of a nineteen-year-old girl who passed on from scleroderma wrote to me about the agony their daughter went through as a result of her illness. The illness causes a very painful breakdown of the skin, and she suffered so much that her mother actually considered killing her so that she could escape the pain—that is how hard it was to watch her suffer. Yet when I discerned her from the hereafter she was remarkably candid about needing to have the experience on the earth, as part of her spiritual education She stated to me (and her parents) that although she wouldn't *"wish that kind of pain on a dog,"* she benefited from that hard lesson so much in the hereafter that, *"If I had to do it again to get the same reward here, I would in a heartbeat."* It sounds amazing, but the souls there who have passed from terminal illness all say the same thing—although the suffering was hard, the second they passed into the hereafter they understood completely why it had to be that way—and are happy they did.

I don't have to tell you why the souls there sometimes refer to this existence as "Hell"—I think you know. We cannot understand it while we are on the earth, but everything we put into this life we get back and more in the next. This life is a small price to pay for the incredible joy and peace of the hereafter—your loved ones there can tell you that.

My fiancé died on October 30, 1997, from a massive heart attack. A month or so earlier we had a discussion about heaven and hell. He believed that he was not going to heaven. He said, "I won't be there when you get there, sweetheart." I argued with him that God is all forgiving and he was a good person. He seemed to believe that he was not a good person and therefore would not be in heaven. Since his death, I've been doing everything to make sure that Tim did make it to heaven. So far, I believe in my heart, but not in my mind. What do I do for peace?

Your fiancé is among the happy souls surrounded by the love and peace of the Infinite Light. How do I know? I know because the souls in the hereafter have told me that *everyone* who passes into the hereafter, regardless of their not-so-perfect behavior on the earth have an opportunity to see the instances in their lives where they could have done better and work toward their spiritual goals in the hereafter. It is called the Life Review. When the souls see their lives through the eyes and hearts of others they affected (good and bad), they understand that it is within their power to learn from past mistakes and work toward peace and true self-understanding in the hereafter. The souls move forward to the Infinite Light because they *want* to—that is all the Infinite Light asks of them. You are right that the Infinite Light is forgiving, because it understands everything and everyone completely. "Hell" is only a state of mind in souls who refuse to take the challenge of growing and learning in the hereafter (and is also very rare).

Sometimes people speak of their lives out of fear—fear of the unknown or fear of what is expected of them when they pass. Funnily enough, these people are the best subjects to discern since they are so happy to prove themselves wrong to their loved ones still on the earth.

So how do you find peace? Pray *for* and *to* your loved one in the hereafter. Just as they have found grace in the Infinite Light, they can bring that grace to us in a special way on our own journey to the Light.

My sister's twenty-one-year-old son committed suicide in her presence a short while ago. She is overcome with grief and worries constantly about his spiritual well being . . . where he is, is he safe, etc. She cannot forget the last moments of his life and constantly relives the scene, which was devastating. We, her family, are at a loss as to how we can help her. She says that if he could just "appear" to her or send her a sign, that she could perhaps begin to live again. Have you any suggestions as to how we may help her?

I do not have to tell you that suicide, or murder of self (as they consider it in the hereafter), is one of the most painful and devastating ways to have a loved one pass. So often the pain of loss is coupled with anger and guilt by a family at odds to understand such a desperate act.

I have come to understand over the years why the hereafter considers suicide a "murder"; it is a desperate act committed by desperate people. The souls who have passed by their own hand tell me that they were not in the right frame of mind prior to passing. This form of psychological turmoil is considered an illness by the hereafter, and those who pass by their own hand are victims of this illness. No one is to blame and no one is blamed.

I know it has been taught in some religions that suicide is a "sin." That is definitely *not* the perspective of the hereafter. Those who have passed by their own hand have told me that the Infinite Light is at its most forgiving and compassionate, and these victims are helped to understand that whatever the turmoil they endured on the earth, it is now over and they are in a peaceful and comforting environment. They only hope that we can understand and forgive as well—they did not want to hurt us, they just lost hope and wanted to end the pain.

Victims of suicide in the hereafter and the victims of suicide here (the family) benefit from the same thing—time, understanding, forgiveness and healing. Through the grace of the Infinite Light, your loved one in the hereafter will gain peace and then also help guide you from his unique perspective there to peace and healing.

Since the death of my mother, my ten-year-old nephew has been having contact with both my mother, and my daughter who passed in December of 1995. He seems to be very genuine about his conversations with them. The problem is that on earth, my mother was a very controlling person, and she and my daughter did not get along very well. My nephew tells us that my mother is taking care of a baby in the dimension where she is, and she has coerced my daughter into taking care of the baby the biggest part of the time. Because what he says seems so genuine, I am concerned, if it is true, for my daughter. I would hate to think of her being taken up in this control there as well as here. This goes against a lot of my basic beliefs about life after death, but since I have never been there, I am torn now. Any insight you can give me would be greatly appreciated.

There are a few issues in your question, so let's go through them one by one.

Firstly, many children do experience some form of communication from the other side, primarily because no one has told them yet that it is "impossible." To these children, it seems perfectly natural, and it is. Often though, some messages might not be interpreted correctly by a child, or the child cannot separate his own reality from that of the hereafter. Listen to the messages, but use your own judgment as far as the content.

That having been said, I can move to the other point of your question, which concerns relationships in the hereafter. In many discernments that I have done for people, they are surprised to hear that their loved one has reunited in the hereafter with an ex-husband or a domineering or abusive relative or friend. To me this is not surprising. In a dimension where total love and forgiveness rule, the souls in the hereafter who were abusive on the earth come to the realization immediately in the hereafter that their actions hurt another, and they want to do whatever they can to make amends. It does not surprise me that your mother and daughter are together— with total understanding of each other's weaknesses and potential to be kind and loving they can now have a relationship of total understanding, acceptance, and love. With respect to the baby your nephew spoke of, it could be the soul of a miscarriage of someone in the family, but my guess is that it is actually a symbol of unity and love between your mom and daughter. Trust me, they are happy and at peace in the hereafter—that is why they are together!

My son died at the age of two and was only just beginning to use words. I've been hesitant about seeking out a medium because of my son's inability to verbalize. How does a very young child come through in a discernment? Are you able to hear them speak or do they only use symbolism?

The souls, no matter what age they are, are always able to communicate. Souls of the unborn (stillbirth, miscarriage, and aborted) are also able to communicate.

The same is true of those who, even as adults, cannot speak. There was a gentleman who came to me concerned that his daughter would not be able to communicate from the hereafter since she was profoundly retarded on the earth. During the discernment, however, she had plenty to say, and explained that without the encumbrance of a body that could not speak, now she was free to express herself. She also added that just because a person cannot speak does not mean that they do not think. She was aware of everything (as are children, also) that went on during her lifetime, even though to the outside world she appeared incoherent. It is really quite astounding, and important to remember when we deal with children, the very old, the mentally ill, and pets, too.

About one month following the tragic sudden death of my thirty-three-year-old fiancé, a psychic medium told my sister that I must "let him go." She said that holding on to his spirit on this "earth plane" would hurt him. The medium said his spirit could get stuck here and he would be in danger of the other bad spirits that were also stuck here lurking about.

Am I really holding him back spiritually by yearning to have his spirit here around me as much as possible?

This almost sounds like a science-fiction plot—nothing could be further from the truth.

I can tell you quite emphatically that the souls are not "stuck" on this earth plane, but can be with us any time we need them. They do this willingly and for as many times as we need them. They understand that eventually, we will come to rely on them less heavily and that we will be able to recognize that they, too, are fulfilling their spiritual journey there as we are fulfilling ours here. During just about every session, the soul in the hereafter has encouraged the family to "pray" for them—a real indication that they enjoy and encourage dialogue from their loved ones. When in doubt about anything someone tells you about your loved ones, always listen to your heart—or ask your loved one in the hereafter!

What do you say to people who see what you do, experience these profound messages, and still don't believe that the souls exist?

I remember watching the movie *Agnes of God* where a young nun tells the story of being touched by St. Michael the Archangel, but is tried for murder after killing the baby she bore, trying to "send it back to God." It was a story of faith—she was either insane, or she had actually been asked by God to endure this struggle. In the end, no one but the young nun is sure.

I cannot explain to people what I have seen, what I have heard, and what I have experienced in communicating to souls who shine so brilliantly in peace and love. I believe in them with all my heart. Like the movie—either I am insane or I have been touched by the souls in my lifetime. Unlike the movie, in the end, all of us will know for sure.

George, you are such an extraordinary man who has helped so many find peace and con-solation. When it is finally your time to follow your own light into Heaven, what would you want the earth to remember about you?

Thank you for your kindness. That has been a running joke among my friends for a long time. They tell me my headstone will the cheapest one in history, because my entire life can be summed up in just five words: "I was just the instrument."

ACKNOWLEDGMENTS

There have been many people who have graced our journey here with their friendship, their generosity, their courage, and their hope. We are profoundly grateful to the following people, both here and hereafter, for sharing their gifts with the earth so that the story of the Garden could be told.

Mary and James O'Reilly, and the soul of Master Colin O'Reilly

Pauline and Dennis Patterson, and the soul of Mr. Jeffrey Patterson

Ms. Susan Marek, and the souls of Master Ryan Marek I and
Master Ryan Marek II

Rosemary and Luther Smith, and the souls of Mr. Drew Smith
and Mr. Jeremiah Smith

Ms. Connie Carey, and the soul of Ms. Michele Carey

Ms. Elaine Stillwell, and the souls of Ms. Peggy O'Connor and
Mr. Denis O'Connor

Ms. Judy Silvers Freedman, and the souls of Fae and Dave
Silvers

Ms. Maria Stalzer and the soul of Ms. Vincenza Barone

Jan and Raine De Leur

The family of Anne Frank

Mr. Brian Patterson

The Sisters, Servants of Mary

Monsignor Anthony Della Villa

Monsignor Thomas Hartman

Ms. Dianne Vitucci and the soul of Mr. Howard Lyons

Mr. Neal Sims

Ms. Emily Max-Oscartu

Risa Gold, M.D., and the Gold family

Daniel and Michelle Zehrer

Mr. Charles Ross

Mr. John Redmann

Ms. Tracy Martin and Mr. Michael Bravin